The Sleep & Evening Routine Sidekick
Journal

Your Guide to a Fulfilling Evening & Rejuvenating Sleep.

Created with love by
Team Habit Nest

Copyright ©2021 Every Damn Day, LLC
All rights reserved.
Published by Every Damn Day, LLC.

No part of this publication may be reproduced, or stored in a retrieval system, or transmitted in any form or by any means, electronic, mechanical, recording, photocopying, scanning or otherwise, without express written permission of the publisher.

For information about permission to reproduce elections from this book, email team@habitnest.com
Visit our website at www.HabitNest.com

PUBLISHER'S DISCLAIMER

While the publisher and author have used their best efforts in preparing this book, they make no representations or warranties with respect to the accuracy or completeness of the contents of this book. The advice and strategies contained herein may not be suitable for your situation. You should consult with a professional where appropriate. Neither the publisher nor the author shall be liable for any loss of profit or any other commercial damages, including but not limited to special, incidental, consequential, or other damages.

The company, product, and service names used in this book are for identification purposes only. All trademarks and registered trademarks are the property of their respective owners.

SPECIAL THANKS

We'd like to extend a wholehearted, sincere thank you to the entire Habit Nest team for helping us create this, from writing to editing to proofreading to formatting. We love ya!

ISBN: 9781950045204

FIRST EDITION

The Habit Nest Mission

We are a team of people **obsessed with taking ACTION** and **learning new things** as quickly as possible.

We love finding the **fastest, most effective ways** to build a new skill, then **systemizing that process for others**.

With building new habits, we empathize with others every step of the way *because we go through the same process ourselves*. We live and breathe everything in our company.

We use our hard-earned intuition to outline **beautifully designed, intuitive products** to help people live **happier, more fulfilled lives**.

Everything we create comes with a mix of **bite-sized information, strategy, and accountability**. This hands you a simple yet **drastically effective roadmap** to build **any skill** or habit with.

We take this a step further by diving into **published scientific studies**, the opinions of subject-matter **experts**, and the **feedback we get from customers** to further enhance all the products we create.

Ultimately, Habit Nest is a **practical, action-oriented startup** aimed at helping others take back decisional authority over every action they take. We're here to help people live **wholesome, rewarding lives** at the **brink of their potential!**

– *Amir Atighehchi, Ari Banayan, & Mikey Ahdoot*
Cofounders of Habit Nest

Table of Contents

1 The 'Why'
- Why Is an Evening Routine So Important?
- Why Is Sleep So Important?
- Sleep as a Performance Activity
- Sleep Deprivation
- Your Immune System
- Your Mental Health Relies on Sleep
- Productivity, Learning, Creativity, and Efficiency
- Understanding Your Why

18 The 'Who'
- The Three Factors of Behavior Change
- Establishing Your Identity
- Remember: Everyone Is Unique

26 What To Expect
- Understanding Your Circadian Rhythm
- Sleep Cycles
- The Impact on Shift Workers
- How Sleep Affects Habit Building
- The Phases of Building a New Habit
- Daily Content

43 The 'How'
- Evening Routine Suggestions
- Common Evening Routine Challenges
- Overcoming Obstacles
- The Most Impactful Strategies for Better Sleep
- Determining How Much Sleep You Need

- *Common Sleep Disorders*
- *Holding Yourself Accountable*
- *Perfectionists, Tread Lightly*
- *Sample Content Page*
- *Sample Journal Page*
- *Commit*

65   *Phase I (Days 1-7)*

83   *Phase II (Days 8-21)*

117   *Phase III (Days 22-66+)*

214   *Fin*
- *So... What Now?*
- *Meet the Habit Nest Cofounders*
- *What Habit Will You Conquer Next?*
- *Share the Love*
- *Content Index*
- *How Was This Journal Created?*

Our Mission for This Journal

This journal is about building two equally important habits:

1. Establishing a consistent, intentional evening routine.
2. Implementing proper sleep hygiene to get the best night's sleep possible.

The truth of the matter is that most people need some form of guidance when it comes to personal development.

Because you bought this journal, you're probably someone who is generally into personal development. You're probably familiar with ordinary journals that promise to help you remain productive, create useful routines, etc.

Throughout the journal, you'll find an abundance of information on both evening routines and sleep.

This journal is a compilation of the best tips and strategies discovered by people who understand the importance of an evening routine and quality sleep. We've dug through many research books, podcasts, scientific studies behind willpower, cool products/apps/gadgets, and dissected successful leaders' strategies to find the golden nuggets of info and present them here.

The result is a journal bringing something new to the table. **Actionable tips** and **motivating content** are what we're all about.

Every day, for 66 days, we're going to give you the information, motivation, and accountability you need to stay consistent in making significant strides towards your goal of bettering yourself.

Why 66 days? In a recent study on human behavior, researcher Phillippa Lally discovered that on average, it takes 66 days to form a habit. In reality, there is no exact, definite, magical moment. But from personal experience, 66 days is a long enough time to build the habit so strongly that you can tap into it at any future point in your life.

Our mission is to be your book-sized personal trainer for building this life-altering habit into your day to day life.

Establishing a solid evening routine can massively impact your sleep and, further, your daily productivity and health. By forming healthy habits in the evening you maximize and amplify the quality of every hour you spend awake.

Your mind might try to fight this change. You might be thinking things like, "Is it even worth trying? Does it really matter to have a routine in the evening? I'm routinized all day, don't I deserve to be free from a schedule at night? My kids definitely won't let me get anything done…"

Remember:
Excuses are the *enemy of your goals*. Excuses are the *enemy of change*. Today we stop making excuses, together.

In this moment, you're already doing something amazing. The fact that you're reading this means somewhere in you there is a burning desire to really add this habit and make it stick.

Let's make it stick and add value to our lives in an amazing, indescribable way.

The 'Why'

Why Is an Evening Routine So Important?

If you're really looking to make the most out of each day, having an evening routine is just as important as a morning routine and your other daily habits.

How many evenings do you find yourself doing these things before bedtime?

- Mentally composing forgotten emails and texts
- Mulling over what happened that day
- Stressing over what's on your plate for tomorrow
- Wiring yourself with snacks
- Staying up late watching TV or scrolling through social media

Without an evening routine, falling into these habit traps is practically inevitable, and it has a bigger impact than we realize in the moment.

By the time evening rolls around, your willpower is sapped. This makes it easy to throw all your hard work from the day out the window and sink into counterproductive habits like eating junk food, parking yourself in front of the TV, and staying up too late. That's not to say that relaxing is bad, but defaulting to these habits can interrupt your sleep and sabotage the day ahead.

With the right routine, your evening can still be relaxing, productive, and set you up for a new, energy-filled day.

Why Is Sleep So Important?

Without realizing it, our society has normalized the deprivation of a MASSIVELY crucial resource: sleep.

Sleep is widely regarded as something we can deal without or skimp on. It's not uncommon to see people pulling all-nighters to work or study, or at the very least, shaving hours off their sleep schedule. No big deal, right?

It's actually a HUGE deal. Every single internal system we have relies on sleep for regulation and recovery. Even our brain's cognitive performance and mental health rely heavily on sleep for optimal performance.

While you sleep, your brain is actually hard at work performing maintenance on your cognitive functions, consolidating your memories, balancing hormone production, and even trying to solve problems you're facing.

To properly put the value of sleep in perspective, our time asleep and our sleep quality is just as valuable for our productivity, health, and social function as our time awake.

Sleep expert Matthew Walker, a professor of neuroscience and psychology, even found that sleep is the most important piece of your health trinity (sleep, nutrition, and exercise).[1]

---

[1] Walker, Matthew. *Why We Sleep*. Penguin Books, 2017, p. 5.

To paint a bigger picture, here's a list of the some of the most notable benefits of sleep to both physical and mental systems:

Physical:

- Blood pressure regulation
- Promotes heart health
- Weight management
- Increased energy
- Supports recovery from illness and injury
- Immune system support
- Hormone regulation
- Supports gut health via your gut microbiome
- Helps manage blood sugar
- Cancer & malignancy prevention

Mental:

- Improves mental health disorders like depression and anxiety
- Increased creativity
- Better focus
- Learning ability improvement
- Memory retention
- Increases your ability to empathize with others
- Better problem-solving skills
- Impulse control and willpower
- Stress management

Sleep as a Performance Activity

How many times have you watched motivational videos that encouraged you to skip sleep if you ever want to be successful?

The "Hustle Culture" is notorious for pushing the idea that part of success is sacrificing your sleep and spending every waking moment working.

Although this might seem like no big deal, cutting down on sleep can actually be detrimental to your productivity and performance.

Getting the right amount of sleep and getting good *quality sleep* can actually **amplify** your performance, and even help you stave off job burnout. This applies regardless of what type of productivity occurs or what your daily activities entail.

Research over the years gives valuable insight into how sleep impacts our performance, both in everyday activities and elite athletic training. Two of the biggest conclusions are:

- Humans need at least 7 hours of sleep for optimal cognitive performance.
- Getting less than 6 hours of sleep each night is a key factor that leads to job burnout.[2]

---

[2] Söderström, M., Jeding, K., Ekstedt, M., Perski, A., & Åkerstedt, T. (2012). Insufficient sleep predicts clinical burnout. Journal of Occupational Health Psychology, 17(2), 175–183. https://doi.org/10.1037/a0027518

This doesn't make self-improvement advice a *bad* thing. Just don't forget to prioritize sleep for your performance, eat healthy, and reduce your stress levels.

Sleep Deprivation

Not only is sleep great for your body and mind, but a lack of sleep is much worse than you might think. To top it off, sleep deprivation is so normalized that most don't realize how impaired they actually are!

According to sleep expert Matthew Walker, participants in a study on sleep deprivation spent 10 nights getting only 6 hours of sleep. Tests done on different areas of their performance showed them to be just as impaired as someone who hadn't slept in 24 hours. Yet, quite surprisingly, most of the participants felt that they were performing just fine.[3]

If the experiment had continued, their performance would have continued to deteriorate even more. Despite the proven detriment to cognitive and physical health, 45% of people only sleep for 6 hours or less.

Performance loss isn't the only blow dealt to us when we deprive ourselves of sleep. Lack of sleep weakens the immune system and raises the risk of a multitude physical and mental health issues like cancer, diabetes, infertility, obesity, stroke, Alzheimers, depression, and heart attacks.

If you shave another hour off to only 5 hours of sleep per night, the risk of death from ***all causes*** shoots up by 15%!

---

[3] Walker, Matthew. Why We Sleep. Penguin Books, 2017

Some examples of disastrous accidents in which being sleepy is partly to blame include[4]:

- The 1979 nuclear explosion at the Three Mile Island power plant in Pennsylvania.
- The 1986 Chernobyl explosion in the former USSR.
- The 1989 Exxon Valdez oil spill near Alaska.

To further put the extent of impairment into perspective, 20 hours of sleep deprivation impairs you just as much as having a blood-alcohol content of 0.08%, which is the legal limit in the United States.

What it all boils down to is that we are wholly dependent on sleep - physically, emotionally, socially, behaviorally, and everything in between!

---

[4] UCLA. "Coping With Shift Work - UCLA Sleep Disorders Center - Los Angeles, CA". Uclahealth.Org, https://www.uclahealth.org/sleepcenter/coping-with-shift-work.

Your Immune System

You've probably experienced this scenario before: After a few days of having your brain and body going nonstop, you start feeling sick. Maybe you stayed up a little too late, got awakened multiple times by kids, or had to wake up earlier than usual. However it happened, your immune system got a little too wiped out!

Your immune system is the best possible defensive and offensive system for your body. It destroys bad bacteria and virus cells, keeps your health in check, and fights cancer cells that attempt to develop. It's a vital part of survival and living a healthy life. The immune system deploys several of its best weapons, including killer T-cells and cytokines, to keep your body in proper working order. Cytokines, especially, are primarily created and released into your system during sleep.

Without adequate sleep, your immune system can't work at full capacity. Obviously, those cytokines that rely on sleep would slow drastically in production. On top of that, research has proven that even one night with only 4 hours of sleep can demolish up to 70% of your crucial killer T-cells.

Imagine if you kept this up for a week? A month? A year? Not only would you become more susceptible to the common cold or the flu, you could be more than doubling the risk of developing cancer!

In terms of health and wellness, your immune system (and therefore, your sleep) deserves a top spot on your priority list. While rough nights are bound to happen (and aren't anything to get too anxious about), your body will thank you for getting good sleep at every opportunity!

Your Mental Health Relies on Sleep

When it comes to sleep and mental health, it can become quite a "chicken or egg" conundrum. It can be hard to pinpoint which came first.

While sleep deprivation has clear ties to conditions like depression and anxiety, being depressed and anxious can lead to insomnia and fragmented sleep. Even if you slept long enough, the fragmented sleep can be enough to root you into fatigue and sleepiness the next day.

While past studies concluded that sleep-deprived people were 5-7 times more likely to feel lonely and helpless[5], research also points to the necessity of adequate REM sleep to heal on an emotional level. REM sleep also aids the way your emotions intertwine with those around you, alleviating some of the social isolation often felt with depression and anxiety. It helps you read others and their emotions more accurately, empathize with them, and communicate better[6].

It may seem an insurmountable task to break the cycle in the beginning, and that's completely okay. That's why you have this journal in your hands. It can be your guide and steady foundation in forming new sleep hygiene habits. Step-by-step, evening-by-evening!

---

[5] Huffington, Arianna Stassinopoulos. The Sleep Revolution. Harmony Books, 2016, p. 28.

[6] Walker, Matthew. Why We Sleep. Penguin Books, 2017

Productivity, Learning, Creativity, and Efficiency

Whether you're working, taking classes, or practicing a hobby, all areas of your cognitive function can benefit exponentially from a well-rested brain. Your brain can even map things out through crazy, amazing problem-solving abilities while you sleep!

Productivity and efficiency stand at the forefront of our daily lives. From the moment we wake up, our clock starts ticking. We may need to meet a project deadline, pitch a new idea, or tackle a massive to-do list. How are we supposed to handle the daily grind when we're stumbling through the entire day with a brain that's still half asleep?

With a well-planned evening schedule and proper sleep, your work effectiveness gets an insane boost. A refreshed brain is better able to focus on, comprehend, and retain information throughout the day. Whatever you then learn and retain from your day is later consolidated and stored during that night's sleep. If you don't bother to get good rest that night, much of that information can, instead, be lost or completely jumbled.

Creativity also blossoms when you've gotten ample sleep. That doesn't just mean the creativity that makes you think of art, music, dancing, or theatre. The abstract thinking of creativity is a valuable cognitive function for any career or ambition.

How valuable is creativity? In 2010, an IBM survey of over 1,500 business executives concluded that creativity was the

number one factor in a business' success.⁷ Creativity was considered more important than even vision, discipline, and integrity! Why is that, exactly?

Well, in a world saturated by so many options for a given product or service, creativity is what creates the competitive edge. Hundreds of markets continue to grow even more saturated compared to 2010, making creativity more valuable than ever. It brings fresh ideas to the table, original concepts that other businesses didn't think of. Creative employees are able to solve problems in brand new ways and think of innovative approaches.

Even more amazing is the fact that the creativity boost isn't just a result of getting more hours of sleep. REM sleep, in particular, promotes creativity by taking seemingly unrelated bits of information, both stored and new, to create connections between them. As a matter of fact, Dmitri Mendeleev started the periodic table of elements after dreaming about it!

---

⁷ IBM. "IBM 2010 Global CEO Study: Creativity Selected As Most Crucial Factor For Future Success". IBM News Room, 2010, https://newsroom.ibm.com/2010-05-18-IBM-2010-Global-CEO-Study-Creativity-Selected-as-Most-Crucial-Factor-for-Future-Success?mhsrc=ibmsearch_a&mhq=2010%20CEO%20Survey.

Understanding Your Why

As humans, what sets us apart from other animals is our desire to be great as opposed to simply surviving. We all have a vision of what our ideal life might look like.

The absolute most important aspect of changing your life for the better is… **Knowing your damn *Why*.**

The thing is, when we forget (and we forget quite often) the reason we're struggling to improve our lives, we tend to retreat to our habitual selves - to the person we were before we made the decision to change.

Having a clear understanding of your 'why' (what you want to change and why you want to change it) is what pulls you through the tough times you will inevitably face when altering your habits.

Here are a few simple questions that **you should take your time to sincerely answer before moving on**.

These questions are aimed at getting to the root of what is driving you to change your evening habits and in what ways you hope it will benefit you.

The point of this is to guide you to make concrete decisions about how to prioritize sleep. It's here to remind you of how these changes get you closer to turning your vision of your dream life into a reality.

If you're going to even make an attempt at this, you better know why you're doing it in the first place.

Seriously. Take the time to define your dream life.

1. What would my life look like if I prioritized conquering my evening routine every single night for the next 30 days?

_____

_____

_____

_____

_____

_____

2. What sort of ripple effect would doing this have on other areas of my life? On other people's lives around me?

___

3. What would my life look like if I do not do this? What might suffer if I don't prioritize my evening routine and, in turn, set myself up for a successful nights' sleep?

___

4. What life goals have been consistently impeded by a lack of good sleep? How will getting better sleep get me closer to my goals?

_____
_____
_____
_____
_____

Bonus Question: What are the top hurdles I'm facing with completing an intentional evening routine and setting myself up for a good nights' sleep? What do I need to do to overcome these?

_____
_____
_____
_____
_____

Bookmark this section and flip back here the next time you're struggling to stay consistent with this habit.

This section is your SOS Lifeline.

The 'Who'

The Three Factors of Behavior Change

James Clear, author of *Atomic Habits*, writes that there are essentially three parts to behavior change (we love your work, James!).

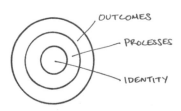

1. The Outcomes

The first is the outside layer, the outcomes. This is synonymous with your goals or where you want to get to, e.g., setting myself up for a good nights' sleep by establishing a quality evening routine.

Outcomes are most useful at setting a larger, over-arching vision for where you want to go to. The downsides of over-focusing on your outcomes are relying on hitting your goals to bring you happiness instead of enjoying the process, and a lack of practicality for what to do day-to-day.

Your outcomes are likely to change over the course of your life to match your ever-evolving goals and needs.

2. The Processes

The second, middle layer, is about processes — this boils down to what system and action steps you put in place to make your outcomes come to be. These are things like I will tell my family about my goal of creating an evening routine and why it's so important to me. I will be disciplined and not allow myself to be distracted during my routine. I will make my sleep-health a priority. This is synonymous with strategies and tactics.

These can be very useful, especially when you find one that clicks, and you'll see a number for you to experiment with sprinkled throughout the journal.

These processes are likely to change over time as you test different ones out, see what works best for you, and switch things up when you get bored / desensitized to them.

3a. Your Identity

This one's the big kahuna. This is the inner-most layer, identifying what your internal belief is of yourself as a person. The biggest mistake people make in enacting behavior change is placing way too large of a focus on the first two parts of this puzzle, while entirely forgetting about the third and the most impactful — how you view yourself.

By properly emphasizing WHO you want to grow into, you will maximize your self-respect, satisfaction, and ability to control your actions — more than any motivation or strategy can give you. Your identity is what you can always fall back on to set your intuition, to guide you to what you should really be doing.

An example of setting your identity is:

"I'm someone who has a calming, fulfilling evening routine that not only sets me up for a good nights' sleep, but an incredible tomorrow."

> *After defining the identity you want to grow into for yourself, chances are this will **not change much**, but rather, only **strengthen over time** based on your actions.*

3b. Your Identity On Your Off-Days

As much as this plays a role in building towards your goals, it's equally as important in regards to times where you fall off the wagon.

Most people subconsciously forget about what their self-identity looks like when this happens, allowing a massive negative self-view to kick in.

This leads to a major emotional factor, **guilt**, to kick in, and as many studies have shown, **guilt is a willpower destroyer** (these are cited at the end of the book).

Instead, mindfully set your identity in these situations. We have two recommendations for this:

> Grow into the person who uses every opportunity of falling off-track to further strengthen your ability to *switch from your off-days back to being on-track.*

Chances are you won't perform an intentional evening routine and have an amazing night's sleep every single day for the rest of your life, right? Life is about knowing which habits to employ, at the right time, to help you get the most fulfillment out of life.

This involves testing different things and seeing how they serve your life's purpose. In order to really do this, you must master the ability to switch back and forth and how to quickly rebuild the momentum you had with your habits, without any guilt that you "lost your mojo."

Be the type of person who can forgive yourself for your mistakes, who will love yourself unconditionally and be a true best friend to yourself (because if you can't, who will?).

We know these are big emphases on emotional states that can come off "fluffy" but the truth is our fulfillment in life directly ties to our emotional states. Learning how to master them is the true feet of this journal, not just building up a specific habit.

Establishing Your Identity

Write your identity statement here.

What kind of person do you want to grow into through this process?

_____
_____
_____
_____
_____

What kind of person do you want to be when you fall off the wagon of your habits? What do you want to remember about who you are and how you can repurpose these days to serve your life?

_____
_____
_____
_____
_____

Remember: Everyone Is Unique

There is nobody else in this world exactly like you. Your mind and body won't respond to the same things that work for your best friend, family member, or neighbor.

As an early 1900s anthropologist, Clyde Kluckhohn, said, "Every human is like all other humans, some other humans, and no other human." Some facts about sleep are concrete and apply to all humans, and you will find some things that work similarly for you as it does for others. Yet, despite the similarities, you are beautifully and uniquely *YOU!*

While science and studies back the effectiveness of many of these methods, they still won't work for everyone. Everyone has a ton of unique, individual evening and sleep needs and factors.

Don't compare your sleep schedule to the schedules of other people. If you're relying solely on doing exactly what someone else does, you only slow your own progress and create frustration.

The best way to find what works for you is to try many different things. It involves a lot of trial and error, but it's the only way to get the best, most effective sleep habits. Try many things, but only keep what works best for you.

What to Expect

Understanding Your Circadian Rhythm

Your circadian rhythm is a natural biological process that regulates your sleep-wake cycles over a 24-hour period. It relies on several factors for regulation, including your body temperature, light exposure, and hormone production.

Disruption of your circadian rhythm is the culprit behind many negative short-term and long-term effects. It's what causes the fatigue or insomnia from jet lag, it can be a factor in depression and anxiety, and it even throws your metabolism out of whack. This is especially common in people who perform shift work (especially with shifts that vary widely) and those that travel often.

Once your circadian rhythm is programmed a certain way, it begins triggering these factors at the programmed time regardless of whether you're ready to sleep or still awake. For instance, your core body temperature would fall and rise at night as it is programmed to do even if you stayed awake all night!

This powerful form of biological programming can be an enemy or a friend. If you've gotten yourself stuck in poor sleep habits and a screwed-up schedule, your body tries hard to stick to it no matter how bad it is. On the bright side, you CAN re-program your circadian rhythm to work *for you* instead of *against you*. That's where your work in this journal really comes into play!

Sleep Cycles

In order to really optimize your sleep, it helps to understand what your brain and body does during sleep!

Your night begins with stage 0, which is your awake time. This includes the time between lying down and falling asleep, as well as brief awakenings throughout the night. These brief waking moments are normal for healthy adults!

Once you start drifting off, you enter stage 1 and transition into stage 2. Stage 1 only accounts for about 5% of your night, while stage 2 accounts for 50%. During these stages, your temperature, heart rate, and breathing begin to decrease. Your muscles start to relax, and might even twitch a bit.

Next, you transition into stages 3 and 4 for about 20% of your night. These stages help prepare you for REM sleep. Stages 3 and 4 are also often referred to as Delta sleep due to the Delta brain waves that would be seen on an electroencephalogram (EEG). Delta sleep is when the major physical restoration occurs. Your body starts healing and regenerating any damaged tissue.

Stage 5 is REM sleep. If you were to view your brain activity on an EEG, it would look quite similar to the amount of activity shown while you're awake! This is the stage of sleep that revitalizes your brain. It is super important for learning, memory consolidation, and problem-solving. During REM, you may have vivid dreams and your body paralyses itself to prevent you from acting out those dreams.

Waking up in the morning or after a nap is easiest during stages 1 and 2. If you struggle to wake up, it might be due to being in the middle of deeper sleep stages. As a general rule of thumb in this situation, it helps to try waking up around 30 minutes earlier.

Let's recap!

- While awake, you are in the "reception" phase of your day. You take in a ton of new information like memories and stuff you learned.
- Non-REM sleep is the "reflection" phase in which you store and build upon the information from the reception phase.
- REM sleep is the "integration" phase. Your brain connects the information, links it to past experiences, builds a mental map of your life, and helps you solve problems.

The Impact on Shift Workers

Having a healthy evening sleep routine to rely on may seem impossible if your job involves shift work. It may not be as straightforward as it is for someone who works the same hours each day, but it can definitely be done!

Rotating shift work is much more common than you might think. About 25% of workers in North America deal with rotating shifts that throw their sleep schedules out of whack.[8]

Most guidelines on sleep hygiene and habits are based on the assumption that your daily schedule is consistent, leaving shift workers without many resources. If you're a shift worker struggling with your sleep schedule, some of these pointers can help you achieve a healthier sleep routine!

- Try to avoid working several night shifts in a row. It can lead you to become increasingly sleep deprived and doesn't give you much time to recover before switching to a different shift.

- If you can't avoid multiple night shifts, try to have scheduled time off before switching to a different shift. This gives you time to get well-rested in-between shifts.

- Ask your employer to give you a consistent cycle of shift rotations that allows a more natural adjustment for your body. The ideal order would be: day shift, evening shift, night shift, morning shift, then repeat.

---

[8] Canadian Centre for Occupational Health and Safety. "Rotational Shiftwork : OSH Answers". Ccohs.Ca, 2020, https://www.ccohs.ca/oshanswers/ergonomics/shiftwrk.html.

- Avoid a long commute if possible. Spending a long time driving takes time away from your sleep and rest times.

- Try to keep your workplace brightly lit to keep you alert while you work.

- If you work a night shift, try exposing yourself to bright light when you wake up to help your body recognize that it's time to be awake and ready to go. Good light sources include special light-therapy lamps or light visors made for people with circadian rhythm disorders.

- It's understandably tempting to drink some coffee or energy drinks during your shifts, but try to limit caffeine. If you load yourself up with caffeine, it can make it harder for you to sleep once your shift is over.

- On your way home, a hat and/or dark wraparound sunglasses to shield sunlight make it easier for you to fall asleep once it's time to hit the hay.

- Communicate with your family and friends. Let them know that your rest and sleep are super important, and ask that they limit texts and phone calls when you're trying to get some shut-eye.

- If you're trying to sleep during the day after a late shift, blackout curtains in your bedroom can make a huge difference. Blocking the sunlight helps signal to your body that it's time for sleep.

- Taking a nap before a night shift - especially if you're sleep deprived - allows you to get refreshed and energized, leading to better job performance. A 90 minute nap is ideal, but any amount is helpful.

- Taking 15-20 minute naps during your work breaks can also promote wakefulness and keep you energized.

How an Evening Routine & Sleep Quality Affect Habit-Building

When it comes to habit-building, we have to realize that our habits are built as a result of chains of actions. If you observe and think about the way you live your life, you'll quickly realize that every action is part of a chain of processes that build off every other action. Decisions interact with each other in ways we don't really pay attention to. For example, if you have a healthy breakfast as opposed to one that might cause some stomach uneasiness, the avoidance of that uneasiness leads to a whole chain of different actions and quality of life.

In the same way, an evening routine that helps prepare for the next day and also helps you get better sleep leads to feeling more energized in the morning, which leads to enhanced decision-making and ability to perform. That enhanced morning quality leads to a better you, and a better you leads to an increasingly better life. In reality, this all happens one decision at a time over a long period of time.

Sleep plays a massive role in creating the stable foundation to build upon. Without it, the part of your brain that controls your impulses and willpower crumbles.

It all starts with a feel-good neurotransmitter called dopamine. Over the course of developing not-so-healthy habits (we all have them), your brain started to associate those habits with a rewarding dopamine rush. That's a huge factor behind how difficult it can be to break bad habits and introduce new ones.

One of the main areas of your brain that is associated with impulsivity and dopamine, the striatum, **_tends to become hyperactive while sleep-deprived_**.

When dopamine tries to lead you astray and your striatum goes into overdrive, your pre-frontal cortex joins the fray. It helps bring impulse control and mindfulness into the equation to keep you on track.

When you skimp on sleep, your pre-frontal cortex becomes slower and less-responsive. One major reason behind this is the fact that your sleepy cells have trouble properly absorbing and using glucose, which is needed to power your brain.

Self-control demands a good chunk of energy, and the limited glucose supply often gets delegated elsewhere to more important tasks.

Getting plenty of great sleep allows your pre-frontal cortex to get refueled and ready for better decisions, while settling down your striatum. It creates an amazing cycle for consistently building better habits during the day simply by getting plenty of shut-eye!

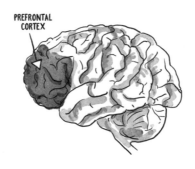

Phases of Building a New Habit

The development of building a habit happens in stages. There's science behind all kinds of different theories about the stages that come along with altering habits, and here's what we found is the most accurate.

Days 1-7, Hell Week.

...*This is going to suck.*

It's going to suck because you're rewiring a lifetime habit to be totally different. Expect HELL. You're likely going to have trouble adjusting to the changes in your pre-bedtime routine. You will NOT easily fall asleep, especially on nights 1 and 2.

This will all fade. Guaranteed. It will fade because your circadian rhythm will adjust and keep your body on track. You'll get used to and start to love your evening routine over time, and you'll begin to naturally get tired when it's time for bed. It won't be easy at first, but your body and mind will learn your evening routine and sleep cues.

But for your brain and body to adapt, you must take action. You must distrust the challenging thoughts your brain will naturally give and show it what you want it to adapt to.

Days 8-21, *Staying Consistent.*

The good news is that after you've gotten through the first week, the process is a lot easier. You've now hopefully figured out a few approaches that work. Your circadian rhythm is catching on to the changes you're making and your brain is recognizing the importance. Your body is slowly growing accustomed to your new hours. You're seeing the benefits of greeting each day well-rested and ready for anything.

During this period, a kick of inspiration can make all the difference. Developing habits takes time and just because you've surpassed the most difficult phase doesn't mean you're off the hook. You'll be learning valuable tips from sleep experts, getting daily challenges to keep you motivated, and learning about some resources that can help you stay on track.

Days 22 - 66, *Hardwiring - Retaining Interest in Your Personal Improvement.*

Once you've passed phase 2, you know for a fact that YOU CAN DO THIS. It's amazing. All it takes is just about a month to add the habit, but that doesn't mean that phase 3 isn't crucial, because it is.

To build a habit means to become mechanical in a certain way. Your mind and your body will be used to your new schedule, you'll know the benefits of a good night's sleep, but you still need to reach the point where there's no thinking about it anymore.

During phase 3 you'll get really cool and interesting tools that you might find useful for mastering your sleep habits. We'll continue to sprinkle in challenges, and other useful info along the way to keep your brain active in making your sleep habits a part of your DNA.

Days 66 and on, **Habit Mastery.**

At this point you've built a solid foundation on which you can continue building and mastering your evening and sleep routine. Even if you won't be sticking to your routine every night — after building this skill, you'll be able to get right back on track when you're ready.

From here, you'll be tweaking and experimenting with different sleep strategies that work best for you. Try different pre-bedtime routines or different hours for going to bed and waking up. You'll eventually find a rhythm and routine that works well for your individual needs. The best part is you'll be navigating this like a pro at this point.

Experimenting can be interesting and enlightening. Feel free to plug in and try new habits that work toward improving your sleep.

The Daily Content

Every single piece of content you're getting is a product of countless hours of sweat and research done by our team to ensure we're doing our best to:

1. Light a fire in you to succeed in adding the habit.
2. Provide you with the necessary knowledge and information to make it simple and easy to get consistently great quality sleep.
3. Make adding the habit fun and interesting.

Not only is every individual piece of content chosen amongst thousands of competing options, but as mentioned in the previous section, the order of the content has been creatively designed to get you through the struggles associated with the different stages of adding habits.

Here are the different types of content you can expect:

Pro-Tips

Pro-tips are the little golden nuggets of information you get to make implementing the habit on a day-to-day basis as simple and painless as possible. The point is to give you expert tips and hacks to get you going, and the variety and diversity of the different pro-tips will provide you with countless options for how to succeed in adding the habit.

Daily Challenges

The daily challenges you'll be receiving will be immensely important to your success in becoming a pro-sleeper.

Why?

They each help target a different area of discipline that will help you force yourself to do what's right, especially when you *don't feel like it*.

By strengthening this willpower-muscle inside you using small, very specific daily challenges, your self-discipline will grow more and more every single day. These daily challenges apply to all other aspects of your life — from curbing negative habits and distractions, to building other healthy habits as well.

Clips & Podcasts

There's nothing quite as motivating as simultaneously seeing the passion in someone's eyes, hearing the truth in someone's voice, and feeling the intensity of their struggle. Connecting with people who have walked in your shoes and crossed over to the light will give you clear reference points that you *can* succeed at this, just as others who have struggled have. Watching or listening to inspirational and informational content will serve as the informative reminder you need to get started and push through your normal, expected struggles until you've mastered this.

Affirmations

Affirmations and visualization are highly effective tools used by some of the most successful people to have ever lived. From athletes, to actors, to CEOs, affirmations are used to help channel positive energy towards goals and create an inevitable connection between your present-self and the end goal you have in mind.

What Affirmations Really Do

1. Subconsciously taps into your creativity-muscle to begin generating creative ways of reaching your goals.

2. Subconsciously programs your brain to associate yourself with the end goal you have in mind, and prepares you to mentally sort out the steps necessary to get from where you

are right now to your end goals.

3. Attracts you to your goal by the simple act of envisioning yourself where you want to ultimately be.

4. Motivates you in the sense that it literally causes your brain to believe that you have within you the power, ability and capability to get exactly where you want in life.

So What Does It Mean to Use Affirmations?

Using affirmations is the act of repeating to yourself that you already are the person you want to be.

It involves envisioning that you can not only achieve your life goals, but that you can be exactly the person you ideally envision yourself to be.

It is the repeating of idealistic situations you would like to see yourself in, except you say them in the present tense, as if they were true now.

While repeating these affirmations, you visualize yourself as this ideal person, in the ideal situation you want to see yourself in, which trains your brain to believe it is possible.

The 'How'

Evening Routine Suggestions

Let's get focused.

There isn't a right answer to exactly how you should set up your evenings. The key is to have a very real understanding of what you want to get out of it.

Your evening routine should bring about a specific outcome in your life. For example, it could be to get better quality sleep and knock out some simple tasks you might have to do early the next day.

To get full clarity on this, write out what you want out of your evenings below. What should they set your next day up for?

_____
_____
_____
_____
_____

Examples of what you can do with your evenings.

For every activity that you put in your evenings, ask if it'll bring about the outcome you identified above or not.

It's also completely okay to experiment here — you can test different activities in your evenings and will likely change these consistently as time goes on.

Here are some popular choices:

- Meditate
- Read
- Write or journal
- Work on a side project
- Get work done that you otherwise have to do later
- Spend time with loved ones
- Do some household chores
- Go for a walk and listen to a podcast
- Make a to-do list for the next day
- Take a bath
- Exercise
- Any small action that might enhance the quality of your sleep

You can create a routine by choosing your favorite actions from the above or creating your own.

You can do whatever you want with your evenings as long as it's furthering your goals, your desires and your life in a way that will positively impact your future.

The whole point of this is being intentional about the way you end your day so you're able to do things that are important to you, and so you can get better quality sleep for the day ahead.

Common Evening Routine Challenge
Doing an Evening Routine When You Live With Others

Doing an evening routine when you have a family or roommate(s) can be a challenge. The best solution here is, of course, to have them join you in making the change!

If the others are not interested in changing their evening routines, which is completely fair and reasonable, there are a couple of action steps you can take to minimize the obstacle of having a different evening/sleep schedule.

After you fill out the 'Why' section in this journal, go ahead and show it to the people you live with. Explain to them how important making this change is to you, and that although you understand if they don't want to join you, you are fully committed to creating the habit of intentional evenings and good sleep hygiene.

Tell them specifically that you would really appreciate if they helped keep you motivated throughout the process and reminded you how important this goal is to you when you're feeling discouraged.

Basically, let them know how much you would appreciate them being a positive force in making this change! The more specific you are about the things that they can do to help, or NOT do that might hurt your chances of performing your new nightly ritual, the easier it will be for them to be the positive force you need.

Your Evening Routine & Sleep vs. Your Social Life

It can seem really difficult to maintain a social life while trying to build a specific nightly routine and get good, quality sleep every night.

As difficult as it may seem, it's doable and actually desired. You always want to have a well-balanced life, and that means avoiding rigidity and making time for important social relationships.

The key here is to be intentional about your evenings even when you have plans at night and won't get to sleep at your usual time.

Here is what you can do:

1. When you have a social event planned on any given evening, still fill out your journal with what your nightly routine will be. Adjust your routine to be much simpler and less time-consuming. Preferably, it should be just a couple of relaxing actions before bed.
2. Plan the amount of sleep you're aiming for based on when you think you'll go to sleep that night.
3. Get right back into your more consistent evening routine and sleep schedule the very next day if possible. The more often you remain consistent, the easier the habit-building process is.

The big secret is.. fill out your journal no matter what. It'll help you remain intentional about this part of your life.

Overcoming Obstacles

It's an unavoidable fact of life: obstacles are going to pop out at you or remain a consistent factor. It could be something unexpected that saps your motivation, a work schedule that makes it difficult to stick to a routine, or having young kids in the house that wake up frequently.

Your path to better habits won't always be a breeze. It takes a lot of dedication and willpower. Some obstacles might even require creative solutions to overcome them.

There's **always** a solution or a way to make it work. Even if the solution isn't perfect, what matters is that you keep trying. Even the smallest of improvements that inch you closer to your sleep habit goals are still so much better than no changes at all. Baby steps in the right direction are better than standing still.

If you can't do an evening routine every night or go to sleep at the same time every night, that's okay. Just do **what you can** to set yourself up for the next day and get the number of hours of sleep you need. Your journey is something to be proud of, not something to feel pressured to do a certain way or ashamed of falling off course.

If some obstacles derail you a bit, remind yourself that it isn't a failure. It doesn't mean you can't get back on track. It doesn't mean that making the changes are impossible for you. It won't be easy, but it will be 100% worth it!

Impactful Strategies for Better Sleep

Without us realizing, some activities during the day can make a big difference in how well we sleep. In the evening, before bedtime, it helps to begin winding down a couple of hours before lying down. Some evening relaxation activities help your body realize that bedtime is coming soon, so it starts getting ready to sleep. Some super helpful and impactful tips include:

- Try to get 15-30 minutes of **direct sunlight** early in the morning
- As it gets closer to bedtime, **start gradually turning off lights in your hous**e. This simulates the gradual darkening of sunlight as bedtime arrives.
- **Make the room as cold as you can stand**. The recommended temperature is 65 degrees, but it's okay if that's too cold for you.
- Wear **warm, fuzzy socks** and warm gloves to keep your extremities from getting too cold.
- Use **blue light blockers** on your phone, computer, and other devices as it gets closer to bedtime.
- Use **heavy blinds or blackout curtains** in your room to block light and help you sleep.
- Drink **as much water as you can** to stay hydrated during the night. Sleeping while even slightly dehydrated can cause your mouth and sinuses to get dry and sore. It can also lead to leg cramps that keep you awake or disrupt sleep.
- **Avoid caffeine a few hours before bed** so it doesn't keep you awake.

- ***Don't eat a huge meal close to bedtime.*** Digestion stimulates your vagus nerve, which is connected to your brain. It's difficult for the vagus nerve to relax after eating.
- ***Avoid alcohol before bed***. It dehydrates you and suppresses your REM sleep. Ideally, you should wait 1 hour per each alcoholic beverage before going to sleep.
- ***Complete workouts early in the day*** rather than later in the evening.

Determining How Much Sleep You Need

Much like everything else, the hours of sleep each person needs can vary widely from person to person. Although you often see 8 hours touted as the standard, the complexity that comes with being a unique human being just can't be boiled down to a one-size-fits-all answer!

Determining your specific sleep needs requires a bit of experimentation over time. It will boil down to a number of factors, both from a genetic standpoint and your external circumstances, like your schedule.

Most of us have to structure our wake-up time around kids or work, which leaves most of the wiggle room down to your bedtime. Once you have a general guideline, you enter a phase of trial and error. Don't put too much pressure on this phase or get stressed if it takes some time!

Recent research leans more toward 7 hours per night as a reasonable benchmark rather than 8. Since sleep cycles are typically around 90 minutes long and you ideally want to complete 5 full cycles, the resulting 450 minutes matches a great in-between starting spot of 7.5 hours to try at the start!

Determine what time you need to be awake in the morning, and then count backward 7.5 hours to determine your bedtime. Pay attention to how you feel in the morning, what time you woke up, and how easy it was to wake up.
If you woke up much easier right around the time you needed to be awake, you've already determined the amount of sleep you need!

If 7.5 hours wasn't your perfect match, don't fret. Make small adjustments of 15-30 minutes to your sleep schedule at a time. If you woke up before your alarm or felt the grogginess of over-sleeping, adjust your bedtime forward a little bit. If you still feel unrested and have a heavy reliance on caffeine to become functional, slowly adjust your bedtime back for a few extra minutes of shut-eye.

Common Sleep Disorders

If you find yourself practicing great sleep hygiene and getting plenty of sleep, but *still* dealing with overwhelming fatigue and sleepiness, an undiagnosed sleep disorder may be the real culprit here.

If you're working against a sleep disorder, you might not make much headway until the root issue is addressed. Checking in with a doctor about unusual long-term symptoms is always a great idea that can give you valuable, often game-changing insights.

Sleep Apnea

An estimated 22 million people in the United States struggle with some form of sleep apnea, with the most common form being obstructive sleep apnea (OSA). Despite being a well-known sleep disorder, it is estimated that 80% of those dealing with sleep apnea go undiagnosed.[9]

Sleep apnea causes episodes of disrupted breathing, causing you to get abnormally low levels of oxygen throughout the night.

OSA can occur for several reasons, but being over the age of 40 and/or overweight are the biggest risk factors. It can also happen to someone young with a normal weight if something else blocks their airway, like enlarged tonsils.

---

[9] American Sleep Apnea Association. "Sleep Apnea Information For Clinicians – Sleep Apnea". Sleepapnea.Org, https://www.sleepapnea.org/learn/sleep-apnea-information-clinicians/.

Typical sleep apnea symptoms include:

- Excessive daytime sleepiness
- Snoring
- Waking up gasping for air or choking
- Other people seeing your breathing stop occasionally while sleeping

Treatment for sleep apnea usually centers around lifestyle changes and devices that keep oxygen flowing while you sleep.

The position you sleep in can help reduce airway obstruction for better sleep. Lying on either side or your stomach is best, but it may be hard to stop yourself from rolling onto your back. Elevating the head of your bed or getting a wedge-like pillow can keep you elevated enough to make a difference. Other people sew items - like tennis balls, for example - onto their pajama tops to thwart their sleepy attempts to roll over!

Insomnia

Insomnia can make it extremely difficult to fall asleep and stay asleep throughout the night. You might find yourself waking up again in the middle of the night unable to fall asleep again. This can lead you to feel:

- Unrested
- Sleepy
- Unable to focus
- Irritable

You can try relaxation techniques like breath work and meditation. White noise machines, soothing waterfall and nature sounds, or light therapy to help you fall asleep. Blocking blue light from electronics closer to bedtime can also be helpful.

Narcolepsy

Narcolepsy is a sleep disorder that messes with your sleep cycles. It causes REM sleep to occur without the other stages of sleep being completed. If the non-REM stages don't properly and fully complete, the physical restoration doesn't get finished. The main symptom of narcolepsy is extreme daytime sleepiness, as well as:

- Episodes of sudden muscle tone loss (which is called cataplexy. Not everyone with narcolepsy experiences cataplexy)
- Sleep paralysis
- Suddenly falling asleep during the day
- Hallucinations

Treatment for narcolepsy usually involves medication to help you stay awake, but good sleep habits and scheduling 1-2 short naps during the day can also help you stay more alert and awake.

Shift Work Sleep Disorder

Shift work sleep disorder can happen to anyone that works odd hours or various shifts that is constantly changing your sleeping and waking schedule.

Not every shift worker develops this sleep disorder, but those who do develop it experience:

- Excessive sleepiness

- Insomnia
- Higher risk of accidents at work or while driving due to the effects of sleepiness

Holding Yourself Accountable
Staying Consistent

One of the best ways to continue doing this habit is to build it alongside a friend who is also passionate about becoming the best version of themselves. Having someone to talk to and brainstorm about your specific pain points makes a huge difference. Their support (and, sometimes, competitive kick) can serve as a nice backup too.

Whether or not that person is also using this journal alongside you, you're still able to work together on establishing a consistent habit together.

If you're the type of person who benefits from a sense of community, we created a free Facebook group specifically designed to hold yourself accountable to using this journal, getting daily support, and for building habits in general.

There's daily activity on there and our team is extremely involved each day.

Join the Habit Nest accountability group here:
facebook.com/groups/habitnest

Perfectionists, Tread Lightly.
The Importance of Not Getting Caught Up With Being 'Perfect' or the 'Best.'

Ideally, we want to have a flawless pre-bedtime routine and hit the sweet spot of how many hours of sleep we get. We'd all love to have a relaxed evening, fall asleep easily, and stay asleep through the night.

But sometimes there's a problem with shooting for perfection from the very start.

Shooting for perfection before you even have time to experiment with your evening routine and sleep needs can prevent you from ever taking one step in the direction of your goal.

So often you see people getting caught up in finding the best way to start working out, the best diet to lose weight, the most up-to-date research on the amount of sleep you need to be getting to feel amazing throughout the day…but we'll let you in on a little secret…

There's one simple concept that shatters all the best research, tips and strategies you can look for (that you'll be getting through this journal).

Here it is… the best way to form a great evening routine and master your sleep habits….

You start doing SOMETHING.

You start taking SOME actions towards your goal.

You make SOME effort.

Don't let the desire to reach perfection disallow you from making sure you make today's evening better than yesterday.

Don't waste your energy fantasizing and searching.

The best way to determine YOUR ideal evening routine is by trying JUST ONE THING.

Nobody ELSE can tell you how to structure your evening for great sleep. All they can do is give you information.

It's up to you to try ONE suggestion, and move forward from that point. Because altering your habits is about investigating what does and doesn't work FOR YOU, not for anyone else.

You'll be getting all the information and motivation you need from us on a daily basis in the form of daily content.

You won't PERSONALLY think every piece of content is useful. You won't think every tip will be effective. You won't think every podcast is insightful. You won't think every affirmation is worthwhile.

But if you make an attempt to use every piece of content, you'll see results. Pinky promise. Disregard the upside you *expect* out of it before trying it — take action first.

Every little action you take propels a snowball effect that greatly impacts other areas of your life.

If you push yourself to have an evening routine for even three days, you're gifting yourself a positive chain of effects that will improve your health, energy levels, cognitive function, and daily productivity. This is the true end goal of getting good sleep, and arguably, of the journal as a whole.

In turn, when you don't prioritize the importance of your evening routine and sleep, each of these things get sacrificed. Building a consistent healthy evening routine is an incredibly powerful tool to help you become the best version of yourself as quickly as possible.

Help your body actually experience this so it has a positive reference point instead of just reading words on this page. Break through every obstacle and excuse you may face to absolutely get to bed early tonight and get good sleep.

Success is all about taking small, consistent actions over time.

Important: **you do not need to finish this journal in 66 consecutive calendar days in order for it to be effective!**

In fact, practically every single person who has tried to build and maintain a habit has failed to follow it at some point.

Instead of trying to gloss over this, we're choosing to take a more practical approach by preparing specifically for those days of failure that will most likely blindside you when you least expect it (e.g. when your motivation is high or something sneaks up on you).

There are two keys to using these struggle days in a way that will benefit you:

First, empathize with yourself in that situation. Don't just think about it, actually feel what you'd be experiencing (e.g. if you were very motivated and one day you slipped up). Put yourself in that headspace.

Second, write out what the most disciplined version of yourself would do in that state, post-failure. Some examples of what your most disciplined self might do:

- Remove all guilt as you realize it's useless. Instead, you immediately search for WHY this happened.

- You get genuinely excited to keep going because you realize that you love challenges - each one you surpass makes you a stronger person.

- This time, you're mentally equipped with all you need to not let this specific mistake happen again.

- You realize this is a completely normal part of the self-improvement process - you gather all your energy, recoup mentally, and attack your day regardless.

Now, for the first time you truly struggle - what would you tell yourself and what would your actions be?

_____
_____
_____
_____
_____
_____
_____
_____

You don't have to do this exactly when you face your first struggle point, but having this as a reference can be extremely useful.

A Simple Idea

We hope that after reading the introductory pages, you're motivated and ready to tackle tomorrow with every ounce of energy you have.

We'll leave you to it with one simple idea.

Tomorrow, you will be exactly who you are **today**.

The rest of your life is a future projection of who you are today.

If you **change** today, tomorrow will be **different**.

If you **don't change** today, the rest of your life is **pre-determined**.

Commit.

No matter what happens tomorrow...

*whether I am exhausted
or have the **worst** day of my life...*

*...whether I win the lottery
or have the **best** day of my life...*

I <u>will</u> make my evening routine and
my sleep a **huge priority** *for the next week.*

*My word is like **gold**.*

I will do whatever it takes
to make this happen.

I <u>will</u> have a productive
evening and sleep routine this week (circle one):

On Weekdays Only   **Every Damn Day**

_____   _____
Signature   Date

PHASE 1:
DAYS 1-7

Phase 1	Phase 2	Phase 3
Days 01-07	Days 08-21	Days 22-66+
Hell Week.	Staying Consistent.	Rewiring Your Brain.

Phase 1: Hell Week

When beginning a new habit, what's really important is getting to the point where you start to see the benefits you expect. It isn't going to be easy to start. You need to believe in yourself and take at least one concrete step in the direction of your goal every single day during this phase because it's really easy to lose hope right off the bat.

Make use of every tip, every affirmation, and all the motivation and information you're getting to make it as easy as possible to take just one action towards your goal every day. Remember, we want to get to the point where we see benefits, and from that point on, self-motivation to re-acquire those benefits comes into play and smooths out the process.

Let's do this.

WAIT! Have you gone through the intro pages of this journal yet? If not, skim through them now! They're quick to go through and imperative to really conquering this habit.

Day 1: **Pro-Tip**

<u>*Make a non-negotiable list.*</u>

One of the best tools for holding yourself accountable to your evening and sleep goals is to prepare a non-negotiable evening routine to complete before bed. There are a couple of reasons why this works so well.

First, being intentional about your evening routine gives you the time and space you need to wind down your day in a way that positively impacts your sleep and overall quality of life.

Second, a big goal here is building a habit of good sleep hygiene. All of our habits are built on each other; they are linked to one another. Creating a routine of non-negotiable actions that become habitual before bed will train you to feel ready to sleep because those actions and your sleep will become increasingly linked together as time goes on.

You'll be writing down an evening routine every time you use this journal. Here's what we recommend as you create your evening routine:

- Be detailed enough that you know exactly what to do
- Be reasonable, not something you know you're unlikely to be able to consistently follow
- Consist of several small tasks, rather than a couple of big, generalized tasks. For example, "take a hot shower, brush teeth, floss…" works better than "get ready for bed."

"Learn from yesterday, live for today, look to tomorrow, rest this afternoon" - Charles M. Schulz

_____ *(Set your lights out time based on when you want to wake up minus your sleep target!)*
DATE

Completed?

💤 SLEEP TARGET FOR TONIGHT: _____ hrs ☐

💡 STRICT LIGHTS OUT TIME FOR TONIGHT: _____ : _____ ☐

WAYS TO IMPROVE MY SLEEP TONIGHT (CIRCLE): *(Check these boxes off when you complete them the next morning)*

| Cold Room (Below 68° F) | Black Out Light Sources | Reduce Blue Light Before Bed | Consistent Sleep Time | No Caffeine After 2pm | No Huge Nighttime Meal | Phone Out of Reach of Bed |

🌙 **MY EVENING ROUTINE FOR TONIGHT:**

1. _____ ☐
2. _____ ☐
3. _____ ☐
4. _____ ☐
5. _____ ☐

💤 **WHAT DO I NEED TO CHANGE IN REGARDS TO MY HABITS WITH SOCIAL APPS / GAMING / ENTERTAINMENT TO IMPROVE MY SLEEP?**

_____

_____

🛏 **SLEEP EXERCISE TO TRY TONIGHT** (OPTIONAL):

PLACE ONE HAND ON YOUR CHEST AND THE OTHER ON YOUR BELLY. SPEND A FEW MINUTES PRACTICING BREATHING DEEPLY INTO YOUR BELLY.

Day 2: **Daily Challenge**

Challenge: Cleanse your room of electronics.

Having your cellphone/tablet/computer in the room can easily disrupt whatever routine you're trying to complete. These devices also make it more likely you'll get lesser quality sleep. Some scientists even think it is potentially dangerous when your electronics are too close to your body throughout the night because of the radio waves they emit.

As you probably already know, T.V. and our cellphones cause us to stay up way longer than intended because of endless content for us to consume. They disrupt our sleep routines and train us to expect to stay up after we get into bed as opposed to being ready for sleep as soon as we get into bed. Even when we wake up in the middle of the night to pick up the phone and check what time it is, notifications can tempt us to check out what's happening in our lives in the middle of our sleep!

Tonight, try ditching electronics in your room, or at least keeping them out of reach and out of sight. If it works well for you, try it for a few more nights. Assess how you feel in the morning, and see if there's an improvement in your sleep and energy levels from this challenge.

"For you to sleep well at night, the aesthetic, the quality, has to be carried all the way through." - Steve Jobs

DATE _____

Completed?

💤 SLEEP TARGET FOR TONIGHT: _____ hrs ☐

💡 STRICT LIGHTS OUT TIME FOR TONIGHT: _____ : _____ ☐

WAYS TO IMPROVE MY SLEEP TONIGHT (CIRCLE):

| Cold Room (Below 68° F) | Black Out Light Sources | Reduce Blue Light Before Bed | Consistent Sleep Time | No Caffeine After 2pm | No Huge Nighttime Meal | Phone Out of Reach of Bed |

(Try each of the above once or twice the first week to see what works for you.)

MY EVENING ROUTINE FOR TONIGHT: ☐

1. _____ ☐
2. _____ ☐
3. _____ ☐
4. _____ ☐
5. _____

HOW DOES MY QUALITY OF SLEEP AFFECT MY MOOD? DOES THIS HAVE ANY SNOWBALL EFFECTS ON MY DAY I SHOULD BE MINDFUL OF?

_____

_____

SLEEP EXERCISE TO TRY TONIGHT (OPTIONAL):

LIE BACK AND CLOSE YOUR EYES. SPEND 5 MINUTES IMAGINING YOUR WHOLE BODY FEELING CALM, HEAVY, AND WARM WHILE REPEATING ALOUD, "I AM COMPLETELY CALM."

Day 3: **Food For Thought**

<u>*Think of sleep as a valuable resource and necessity.*</u>

We often view sleep as something unimportant, something we can do without. We see it as something that isn't nearly as valuable as our time awake.

Considering how sleep amplifies and improves our performance on every level, why don't we value it enough? Why do we often go without sleep so we have more time to be "productive" even though we aren't nearly as functional during our waking hours when we lack sleep?

Next time you are tempted to skimp on the Zs in order to get something done, try to think about all the ways that it could actually hinder your progress. It could make it harder for you to learn, diminish your problem-solving abilities, make it hard for you to focus, or stunt your creativity.

Whatever you're trying to accomplish in your time awake, sleep is one of the important factors that allow you to complete tasks with amazing quality and efficiency. Think of it that way, and treat it that way.

"Properly appraised, our sleeping time is as valuable a commodity as the time we are awake." - Arianna Huffington

_____

DATE

Completed?

SLEEP TARGET FOR TONIGHT: _____ hrs ☐

STRICT LIGHTS OUT TIME FOR TONIGHT: _____ : _____ ☐

WAYS TO IMPROVE MY SLEEP TONIGHT (CIRCLE):

| Cold Room (Below 68° F) | Black Out Light Sources | Reduce Blue Light Before Bed | Consistent Sleep Time | No Caffeine After 2pm | No Huge Nighttime Meal | Phone Out of Reach of Bed |

MY EVENING ROUTINE FOR TONIGHT:

1. _____ ☐
2. _____ ☐
3. _____ ☐
4. _____ ☐
5. _____ ☐

WHAT EXTRA PREP-WORK CAN I DO TONIGHT THAT WOULD IMPROVE MY DAY TOMORROW?

(Think: What can I get out of the way tonight?)

_____

_____

SLEEP EXERCISE TO TRY TONIGHT (OPTIONAL):

LIE BACK AND CLOSE YOUR EYES. FROM YOUR TOES TO THE TOP OF YOUR HEAD, FOCUS ON ONE MUSCLE GROUP AT A TIME. TIGHTEN THE MUSCLES FOR 15 SECONDS, THEN RELEASE AND RELAX THEM FOR 30 SECONDS.

Day 4: **Daily Challenge**

Challenge: Create an optimal sleep sanctuary.

Your sleep space is best reserved for sleeping only. We generally don't think about what we do in each room of our house. You might have a habit of watching TV, working, or studying in your bedroom.

For you to feel fully comfortable and ready to sleep, try turning your bedroom into a sleep sanctuary. Your bedroom should be a barrier where everything from the rest of the day gets left outside of that door.

It all comes down to our biological programming. When we associate our bedroom with activities other than sleeping, we're not optimizing our sleep because we're not being programmed to be physically and mentally prepared for bed when we enter the bedroom to go to bed.

Create a sleep environment that makes you feel comfortable, cozy, secure, and ready to relax. Set it to a comfortable temperature, fill it with your favorite relaxing items, use soothing sounds or music. How you create your sleep sanctuary is up to you, but make it for sleep.

"O bed! O bed! Delicious bed! That heaven upon earth to the weary head." - Thomas Hood

(Journal hack: If you use this journal's elastic band to hold it closed, the band doubles up as a pen holder. Slide your pen clip through it, allowing your pen to rest on top of the book!)

_____
DATE

Completed?

SLEEP TARGET FOR TONIGHT: _____ hrs ☐

STRICT LIGHTS OUT TIME FOR TONIGHT: _____ : _____ ☐

WAYS TO IMPROVE MY SLEEP TONIGHT (CIRCLE):

| Cold Room (Below 68° F) | Black Out Light Sources | Reduce Blue Light Before Bed | Consistent Sleep Time | No Caffeine After 2pm | No Huge Nighttime Meal | Phone Out of Reach of Bed |

MY EVENING ROUTINE FOR TONIGHT:

1. _____ ☐
2. _____ ☐
3. _____ ☐
4. _____ ☐
5. _____ ☐

WHAT'S SOMETHING ON THE BACK OF MY MIND THAT'S STRESSING ME OUT AND WHAT CAN I DO TO ADDRESS IT TOMORROW?

_____
_____

SLEEP EXERCISE TO TRY TONIGHT (OPTIONAL):

LIE BACK AND CLOSE YOUR EYES. STARTING FROM YOUR LOWER BODY ONE MUSCLE GROUP AT A TIME, FOCUS ON THE SENSATIONS, TENSION, AND PAIN YOU FEEL. BREATHE THROUGH THEM AND RELAX YOUR MUSCLES. CONTINUE THE EXERCISE AS YOU PROGRESS THROUGH YOUR UPPER BODY.

Day 5: **Pro-Tip**

<u>*Consistency is the key.*</u>

The best way for your body to stay in a healthy circadian rhythm and develop better habits is for you to be ***as consistent as possible***.

Without consistency, your brain doesn't get the chance to settle into a rhythm, and you basically live in a constant state of jet lag. Having a sleep schedule that is consistent allows your circadian rhythm to naturally mold itself. Once your circadian rhythm is on board with the schedule, it becomes a biological pattern that you can stick to naturally without thinking about it. That's how some people can wake up at the same time every day without an alarm.

This consistency does require some boundaries. Realistically, some events and occasions call for staying up a little later than usual. When it comes to that, it all comes down to maintaining a personal balance that fits your life and works best for you.

In this process, experimentation is needed. While you experiment with what will help you sleep and balance your evenings, nights, and days out, it might feel like your evening routine isn't very consistent. ***What matters most is that you try to keep the times that you go to bed and wake up as consistent as you can.***

"Without enough sleep, we all become tall two-year-olds." - JoJo Jensen

DATE _____

Completed?

SLEEP TARGET FOR TONIGHT: _____ hrs ☐

STRICT LIGHTS OUT TIME FOR TONIGHT: _____ : _____ ☐

WAYS TO IMPROVE MY SLEEP TONIGHT (CIRCLE):

| Cold Room (Below 68° F) | Black Out Light Sources | Reduce Blue Light Before Bed | Consistent Sleep Time | No Caffeine After 2pm | No Huge Nighttime Meal | Phone Out of Reach of Bed |

MY EVENING ROUTINE FOR TONIGHT:

1. _____ ☐
2. _____ ☐
3. _____ ☐
4. _____ ☐
5. _____ ☐

WHERE DO I WANT TO VISIT IN MY DREAMS TONIGHT?

_____

_____

SLEEP EXERCISE TO TRY TONIGHT (OPTIONAL):

LIE BACK AND CLOSE YOUR EYES. VISUALIZE YOURSELF IN A CALM, PEACEFUL PLACE. IMAGINE THE SIGHTS, SOUNDS, SMELLS, TASTES, AND PHYSICAL SENSATIONS FOR AS LONG AS YOU WANT.

(Sleep Exercises are meant to help you mentally and physically relax. No distractions while trying these!)

Day 6: **Daily Challenge**

Try doing your 3 MITs first thing in the morning.

If you find yourself stressing about everything you need to do tomorrow, jot down your 3 MITs (most important things).

Your MITs are the 3 tasks for tomorrow that are ***your top priorities.***

Plan on completing your 3 MITs first thing in the morning. By accounting for these tasks - which may be extremely important, difficult, or time-consuming - you get to relax your mind with the knowledge that they will get taken care of.

With your MITs planned out, you'll likely experience greatly reduced stress and anxiety about the upcoming day, allowing you to be fully present in your evening.

Actually completing your MITs first thing in the morning creates an incredible atmosphere for your day because knocking out three very important or difficult tasks makes you feel beyond accomplished before the day even begins.

Here are the action steps you can take:

1. Write down your 3 MITs the night before
2. Put them in order of most difficult to easiest
3. In the morning as soon as you're mentally prepared, begin knocking them out.

What we're suggesting as a challenge here is basically the opposite of procrastination. Front-load your bigger/more important tasks and take the rest of the day on a lighter not.

"Rest when you're weary. Refresh and renew yourself, your body, your mind, your spirit." - Ralph Marston

DATE _____

Completed?

🛏️ SLEEP TARGET FOR TONIGHT: _____ hrs ☐

💡 STRICT LIGHTS OUT TIME FOR TONIGHT: _____ : _____ ☐

WAYS TO IMPROVE MY SLEEP TONIGHT (CIRCLE):

| Cold Room (Below 68° F) | Black Out Light Sources | Reduce Blue Light Before Bed | Consistent Sleep Time | No Caffeine After 2pm | No Huge Nighttime Meal | Phone Out of Reach of Bed |

MY EVENING ROUTINE FOR TONIGHT:

1. _____ ☐
2. _____ ☐
3. _____ ☐
4. _____ ☐
5. _____ ☐

WHAT DO I WANT TO TELL MYSELF FIRST THING WHEN I WAKE UP TOMORROW?

(What words would set the best tone for the day?)

_____

_____

SLEEP EXERCISE TO TRY TONIGHT (OPTIONAL):

INHALE GOOD, EXHALE BAD DURING DEEP BREATHING. WHILE INHALING, SAY A MANTRA SUCH AS "INHALE RELAXATION." DO THE SAME FOR YOUR EXHALE. FOR EXAMPLE, "EXHALE TENSION."

Phase 1 Complete!

Day 7: **Affirmations**

Worthy of rest.

1. Find a quiet area where you can do this in private so you can be at ease. If you can't find a private space, say this in your head.
2. Think of a time when you felt absolutely relaxed, calm, and pleasant.
3. As you say the following words, imagine yourself in a place that makes you feel incredibly at ease.

I did everything I could do today, and I did my best. I have nothing left to do, nowhere left to go, and it is time to rest. It is time for me to practice self-care and give my body and mind the peaceful sleep they deserve.

Repeat this **one more time.**

"Learning to let go should be learned before learning to get."
- Ray Bradbury

Pssssttt... We like rewarding people (like you) who TAKE ACTION and actually use this journal. Email us now at secret+sleep@habitnest.com for a secret gift ;)

Completed?

SLEEP TARGET FOR TONIGHT: _____ hrs ☐

STRICT LIGHTS OUT TIME FOR TONIGHT: _____ : _____ ☐

WAYS TO IMPROVE MY SLEEP TONIGHT (CIRCLE):

| Cold Room (Below 68° F) | Black Out Light Sources | Reduce Blue Light Before Bed | Consistent Sleep Time | No Caffeine After 2pm | No Huge Nighttime Meal | Phone Out of Reach of Bed |

MY EVENING ROUTINE FOR TONIGHT:

1. _____ ☐
2. _____ ☐
3. _____ ☐
4. _____ ☐
5. _____ ☐

WHAT OBSTACLES DO I FORESEE GETTING IN THE WAY OF HAVING A GREAT NIGHT'S SLEEP TONIGHT? (THINK: WHAT DO I NEED TO AVOID DOING?)

_____
_____

SLEEP EXERCISE TO TRY TONIGHT (OPTIONAL):

SPEND A MINUTE OR TWO HUMMING TO YOURSELF. IT SOOTHES YOUR NERVOUS SYSTEM AND RELAXES YOUR FACE, NECK, AND SHOULDERS.

~~PHASE 1:~~ CONQUERED.

Phase 1 Recap: Days 1-7

1. After looking at your tracking information for Phase 1, what have you learned about your relationship with sleep?

_____
_____

2. What sleep-promoting techniques have you tried that you plan to keep using?

_____
_____

3. What techniques didn't work well for you that you don't plan to keep using?

_____
_____

4. What new techniques do you plan to try in the upcoming days, and how do you hope these techniques will help you?

_____
_____
_____

PHASE 2:
DAYS 8-21

 Phase 1 | **Phase 2** | Phase 3

Days 01-07
Hell Week.

**Days 08-21
Staying Consistent.**

Days 22-66+
Rewiring Your Brain.

Phase 2: Digging Deep - Staying Consistent

Congratulations, you've gotten through Phase 1 (Hell Week).

If you don't feel like you've made as much progress as you'd like, don't worry. One day and one victory at a time is the key.

Phase 2 is important because this is the point where we either feel like we've got it down, OR we feel hopeless that we'll never reach our goals. Either way, ignore what your mind says. If you feel like you've reached your goal, don't trust the feeling because now you need to STAY consistent.

If you feel hopeless, you won't feel hopeless forever as long as you continue to believe in yourself and make a real effort daily.

Commit.

*I KNOW this next phase
is going to be extremely hard.*

*I understand I may not
be perfect about it every day.*

*But I <u>will</u> put my heart, each day, into
conquering this life-changing goal.*

*If I miss a day,
I will pick back up.*

*Off days and missed days
will NEVER stop me.*

*In the long-run,
I will win.*

_____

I <u>will</u> complete Phase 2 of this journal.

_____   _____
Signature   Date

Phase 1 Medal Earned!

Day 8: **Daily Challenge**

Challenge: Avoid sugar in the evening.

No matter how tempting it might be to have a sugary snack before climbing into bed, keep your willpower in check and avoid it as often as possible.

Not only does sugar make you feel wired and disrupt sleep, the combination of sugar and poor sleep leads to a slippery slope of weight gain and blood pressure issues.

The more sleep-deprived you are, the more your hormones get thrown out of whack. Your body no longer metabolizes sugar properly, plus your appetite increases and it takes longer for you to feel full.

Don't let yourself fall into the cycle of sugary snacks and poor sleep! Tomorrow evening, avoid eating any sugary snacks within at least 2 hours of your bedtime. Try to carry this on as another positive habit for your health and well-being!

"Sleep is an investment in the energy you need to be effective tomorrow."
- Tom Roth

DATE _____

Completed?

🛏️ SLEEP TARGET FOR TONIGHT: _____ hrs ☐

💡 STRICT LIGHTS OUT TIME FOR TONIGHT: _____ : _____ ☐

(Get your thoughts out of your head and onto the paper. It enhances positive thoughts and can reduce the effects of negative thoughts.)

✏️ **OPENING UP ABOUT MY DAY:**

_____

_____

_____

☁️ **MY EVENING ROUTINE FOR TONIGHT:**

1. _____
2. _____
3. _____
4. _____
5. _____

(Feel free to incorporate your favorite parts from the previous section's "Ways to improve my sleep tonight" into your evening routine prep moving forward)

💔 **HOW DID I POSITIVELY IMPACT SOMEONE ELSE TODAY?**

_____

_____

🛌 **SLEEP EXERCISE TO TRY TONIGHT** (OPTIONAL):

TRY DRINKING A CUP OF WARM, CAFFEINE-FREE HERBAL TEA THAT PROMOTES SLEEP. FOR EXAMPLE: CHAMOMILE, MINT, OR LAVENDER TEAS.

Day 9: **Favorite Resources**

Try nasal strips.

Note: we have no affiliation with these companies or products, we just think they are great tools.

Do you tend to breathe through your mouth or snore when you're asleep? Breathing through your mouth can be problematic because you may not be getting enough oxygen and, if it's bad enough, that can cause major next-day fatigue. It can also cause your mouth and throat to dry up, which then causes issues like:
- Throat soreness
- Bad breath
- Gum disease
- Tooth decay

Breathing through your nose allows for more oxygen intake, improving your sleep **and** your overall well-being. Try breathing through your nose for a night and see how it impacts your sleep and how refreshed you feel.

If you have trouble breathing through your nose at night, try nasal strips. They work by gently pulling the sides of your nose open to widen the nasal passages.

Tonight, search "nasal strips" on Amazon to check out some product options. Most options are between $10-$15. They're generally comfortable to use, and they're worth a shot for a huge difference in sleep quality!

"A ruffled mind makes a restless pillow." - Charlotte Bronte

DATE: _____

Completed?

SLEEP TARGET FOR TONIGHT: _____ hrs ☐

STRICT LIGHTS OUT TIME FOR TONIGHT: _____ : _____ ☐

OPENING UP ABOUT MY DAY:

_____
_____
_____

MY EVENING ROUTINE FOR TONIGHT:

(Your evening routine should incorporate a mix of utility & calm.)

1. _____ ☐
2. _____ ☐
3. _____ ☐
4. _____ ☐
5. _____ ☐

WHY IS SLEEPING WELL TONIGHT SO IMPORTANT FOR MY DAY TOMORROW?

(The more specific you are, the more you'll feel the importance.)

_____
_____

SLEEP EXERCISE TO TRY TONIGHT (OPTIONAL):

WHILE LYING IN BED, BLINK RAPIDLY FOR 1-2 MINUTES. THIS TIRES YOUR EYES AND HELPS YOU FALL ASLEEP FASTER.

Day 10: **Pro-Tip**

<u>**Blue light blockers.**</u>

Compared to other colors of light, blue light is a short-wavelength light that is massively disruptive to sleep.

Most devices with a screen, like computers or cell phones, give us heavy doses of this blue light.

Blue light is proven to delay the production of melatonin, which disrupts the circadian rhythm. In one study, people that were exposed to blue light felt less sleepy, and they even still felt just as alert late in the evening as they were during the day.

Blocking blue light once the sun goes down helps your circadian rhythm stay on track. Most electronic devices have settings that turn off the blue light.

Another good option is getting a pair of glasses with lenses that are made to block blue light (there are tons of good options out there) and wearing them while looking at screens in the hours before bed.

You might also want to check out light bulbs that help filter blue light!

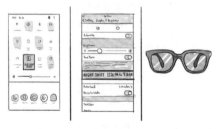

"I want to look at how we can build a path forward for our lives, which is more sustainable and less fueled by burnouts, sleep deprivation, exhaustion." - Arianna Huffington

_____
DATE

Completed?

SLEEP TARGET FOR TONIGHT: _____ hrs ☐

STRICT LIGHTS OUT TIME FOR TONIGHT: _____ : _____ ☐

OPENING UP ABOUT MY DAY:

_____

_____

_____

MY EVENING ROUTINE FOR TONIGHT:

1. _____ ☐
2. _____ ☐
3. _____ ☐
4. _____ ☐
5. _____ ☐

WHAT IS SOMETHING I DO DURING THE DAY THAT AFFECTS MY EVENING ROUTINE/SLEEP QUALITY? HOW CAN I CHANGE IT?

_____

_____

SLEEP EXERCISE TO TRY TONIGHT (OPTIONAL):

LIE DOWN AND CLOSE YOUR EYES. BEGIN DOING ANY LIGHT STRETCHES THAT FEEL GOOD TO YOU. AS YOU STRETCH, THINK ABOUT THINGS YOU WERE GRATEFUL FOR TODAY AND SOMEONE YOU NEED TO FORGIVE.

(Keep an open mind with these. Not every exercise will work for you, but some will be extremely useful.)

Day 11: **Favorite Resources** 🔧

<u>Recommended app: Shortcuts for iPhone.</u>

The *Shortcuts* app for Apple iOS devices allows you to automate a string of actions, which can be useful for automating your evening routine.

Custom evening or bedtime shortcuts can enable or disable certain functions on your phone, begin meditations or music, silence notifications, and more. Any string of commands you can think of can be created through the *Shortcuts* app.

The app also has a library of pre-made shortcuts that you can browse and apply to your phone, making bedtime routines easier to keep up with and adhere to.

Automating parts of your bedtime ritual help your body adjust to that habit and it soon becomes more natural since your brain starts to associate the string of commands with bedtime and sleep.

The only downside to this app is that it isn't available on Android devices.

"Eat healthily, sleep well, breathe deeply, move harmoniously."
- Jean-Pierre Barral

DATE _____

Completed?

🛏️💤 SLEEP TARGET FOR TONIGHT: _____ hrs ☐

💡 STRICT LIGHTS OUT TIME FOR TONIGHT: _____ : _____ ☐

✏️ **OPENING UP ABOUT MY DAY:**

_____

_____

_____

🌙 **MY EVENING ROUTINE FOR TONIGHT:**

1. _____ ☐
2. _____ ☐
3. _____ ☐
4. _____ ☐
5. _____ ☐

💗 **WHAT AM I REALLY HAPPY ABOUT IN MY LIFE?**   *(Reminder: You **always** have more to be grateful for than not.)*

_____

_____

🛌 **SLEEP EXERCISE TO TRY TONIGHT** (OPTIONAL):

WHEN YOU'RE IN BED AND READY TO SLEEP, COUNT BACKWARD FROM 100 TO SEE IF IT HELPS YOU FALL ASLEEP FASTER.

Day 12: **Pro-Tip**

Combatting racing thoughts.

Worries, racing thoughts, and anxiety can get you stuck in a big pile of negativity quicksand. It becomes hard to remove yourself from it and keeps you in a state of panic.

Next time you find yourself struggling with racing thoughts, try this visualization technique to quiet your mind:

- **Close your eyes** and let yourself visualize whatever comes to mind - not just words, but an actual image. Pay attention to all the details, explore it, allow yourself to wonder how it will change.
- **Let your mind focus** on it completely. Allow the visualization to become more clear, more detailed, and more sharp. Sink deeper into the trance created by this visualization.
- **Generate random items** from your racing thoughts and refocus them into something that helps you relax. For instance, visualize shooting those items into the air as if they shot from a cannon.
- **Continue this visualization technique** and fall deeper and deeper into the trance. Eventually, you should become relaxed enough to fall asleep.

"Don't fight with the pillow, but lay down your head, and kick every worriment out of the bed." - Edmund Vance Cooke

DATE _____

Completed?

SLEEP TARGET FOR TONIGHT: _____ hrs ☐

STRICT LIGHTS OUT TIME FOR TONIGHT: _____ : _____ ☐

OPENING UP ABOUT MY DAY:

_____
_____
_____

(What are you going through that would be aided by a shift in perspective?)

MY EVENING ROUTINE FOR TONIGHT:

1. _____ ☐
2. _____ ☐
3. _____ ☐
4. _____ ☐
5. _____ ☐

WHAT DO I NEED TO CHANGE IN REGARDS TO MY HABITS WITH SOCIAL APPS / GAMING / ENTERTAINMENT TO IMPROVE MY SLEEP?

_____
_____

(Even if this is really repetitive, it's worthwhile writing it over and over until you FEEL how important it is.)

SLEEP EXERCISE TO TRY TONIGHT (OPTIONAL):

TRY SOME REVERSE PSYCHOLOGY ON YOUR BRAIN BY REPEATEDLY TELLING YOURSELF TO STAY AWAKE. THIS IS CALLED "PARADOXICAL INTENTION."

Day 13: **Daily Challenge**

Challenge: Scale back on caffeine.

Although caffeine can give you a nice energy boost, too much caffeine consumption can work against your sleep habit efforts.

If you consume a ton of caffeine throughout the day, try these gradual steps to cut down:

- **For the first week**, carry on consuming caffeine like normal, BUT keep track of your caffeine intake using a log. Include ALL caffeine-containing items like tea, chocolate, and headache medications.
- **After the first week**, work on lowering your intake bit by bit. Cut back by around 40 mg of caffeine per day. When choosing what to cut down on, start with the items you consume closest to bedtime.
- **Once you become accustomed to lower caffeine levels**, try substituting other caffeinated items with lower-caffeine, healthier options. For instance, try replacing your caffeinated soda with black tea, which has less caffeine.

Over time, you will be taking in significantly less caffeine. Keep in mind that other forms of caffeine besides coffee generally don't come with as much of a high, or as much of a low.

"In the end, winning is sleeping better." - Jodie Foster

_____
DATE

(Are you experimenting with how much sleep you need for a good day? What have you learned? What can you try with the aim of learning about yourself?)

Completed?

SLEEP TARGET FOR TONIGHT: _____ hrs ☐

STRICT LIGHTS OUT TIME FOR TONIGHT: _____ : _____ ☐

OPENING UP ABOUT MY DAY:

_____
_____
_____

MY EVENING ROUTINE FOR TONIGHT:

1. _____ ☐
2. _____ ☐
3. _____ ☐
4. _____ ☐
5. _____ ☐

HOW DOES MY QUALITY OF SLEEP AFFECT MY MOOD? DOES THIS HAVE ANY SNOWBALL EFFECTS ON MY DAY I SHOULD BE MINDFUL OF?

_____
_____

SLEEP EXERCISE TO TRY TONIGHT (OPTIONAL):

DO A "BRAIN DUMP" BEFORE BED BY JOTTING DOWN EVERYTHING ON YOUR MIND. THIS HELPS YOU GO TO BED WITH A CLEAR HEAD.

Day 14: **Food For Thought**

<u>Your evening willpower.</u>

Breaking old habits and creating new, healthier habits requires a ton of willpower. Impulse control and the ability to keep yourself on track is vital to your success.

But willpower isn't always something you can generate on your own. It involves biological factors, such as natural patterns of brain activity.

Naturally, your *willpower is at its highest in the morning. It gradually lessens throughout the day,* leaving you most vulnerable at night. The more exhausted you are, the less willpower is left for you at night. Diminished willpower leaves you more vulnerable to breaking away from your new sleep habits and routine.

Part of fighting temptation and lack of willpower is knowing about the fact that it is lower at night. When you're mindful of this fact, you can make more conscious decisions rather than act on impulse.

Stay mindful, thoughtful, and determined to stick with your routine. Don't let this natural pattern throw you off course!

"He that can take rest is greater than he that can take cities"
- Benjamin Franklin

DATE _____

Completed?

SLEEP TARGET FOR TONIGHT: _____ hrs ☐

STRICT LIGHTS OUT TIME FOR TONIGHT: _____ : _____ ☐

OPENING UP ABOUT MY DAY:

_____

_____

_____

MY EVENING ROUTINE FOR TONIGHT:

1. _____ ☐
2. _____ ☐
3. _____ ☐
4. _____ ☐
5. _____ ☐

WHAT EXTRA PREP-WORK CAN I DO TONIGHT THAT WOULD IMPROVE MY DAY TOMORROW?

_____

_____

(What small action would make tomorrow morning just a little bit more smooth?)

SLEEP EXERCISE TO TRY TONIGHT (OPTIONAL):

SPEND A FEW MINUTES READING A PAPERBACK OR HARDCOVER BOOK. ONLY PHYSICAL COPIES, NO E-BOOKS!

Day 15: **Daily Challenge**

<u>Challenge: The "chairman of the board" exercise.</u>

If you struggle in the evening with hushing several voices in your head, switch things up and use it to your advantage. You can do this using the "Chairman of the Board" exercise.

Allow each voice to be personified and assume that they have positive intent. Sit them down for a meeting as if you are leading a board meeting. Listen to them, let them teach you or give you feedback. Try to figure out what they need and the reason behind what they say.

Continue this exercise until you have addressed each voice. Once you understand each voice, you can close out the meeting. Use the feedback and information to address those situations in a positive and constructive way.

Taking the voices in your head as separate from you (i.e. not your own active thinking) helps reduce their control over you.

"It is a common experience that a problem difficult at night is resolved in the morning after the committee of sleep has worked on it."
- John Steinbeck

_____

DATE

Completed?

🛏️ SLEEP TARGET FOR TONIGHT: _____ hrs ☐

💡 STRICT LIGHTS OUT TIME FOR TONIGHT: _____ : _____ ☐

(What activities do you want to pay attention to that may be affecting your energy levels?)

✏️ **OPENING UP ABOUT MY DAY:**

_____

_____

_____

☁️ **MY EVENING ROUTINE FOR TONIGHT:**

1. _____ ☐
2. _____ ☐
3. _____ ☐
4. _____ ☐
5. _____ ☐

💤 **WHAT'S SOMETHING ON THE BACK OF MY MIND THAT'S STRESSING ME OUT AND WHAT CAN I DO TO ADDRESS IT TOMORROW?**

_____

_____

🛏️ **SLEEP EXERCISE TO TRY TONIGHT** (OPTIONAL):

LIE ON YOUR BACK WITH YOUR ARMS RELAXED BY YOUR SIDES. FACE ONE PALM TOWARD THE GROUND AND ONE TOWARD THE CEILING. VISUALIZE SLEEPINESS ENTERING THROUGH YOUR UPTURNED PALM, AND EVERYTHING THAT HINDERS YOUR SLEEP EXITING THROUGH YOUR OTHER PALM.

Day 16: **Pro-Tip**

Communicate about your sleep schedule.

Communicating about your changes with your friends and family because it provides a sense of accountability for sticking with your goal and helps alert them not to disrupt your plans.

- If you are making changes to your schedule that affect social plans, let those **friends** know that you are trying to create a better routine and form good habits.
- If **other people in the house** are loud while you are winding down or trying to sleep, communicate with them about the importance of sticking to your routine and getting good sleep
- If **people are frequently calling, texting, or messaging** you during your rest time, let them know that you might not answer after a certain time and ask that they respect and understand that
- If **you share a bed or room** with someone else, talk to them about your routine and habit changes. See if they would be willing to make changes as well, or at least support your decision to change.

Communication is so very important. It helps those around you to understand what you're doing and why you're doing it, making it more likely to respect and support your efforts. Maybe you can convince them to improve their habits as well!

Use this as a call to action to have that difficult conversation with someone that will drastically improve your sleep, such as an obnoxious neighbor or your significant other who may be waking you without them knowing.

"Your life is a reflection of how you sleep, and how you sleep is a reflection of your life." - Dr. Rafael Pelayo

DATE _____

Completed?

SLEEP TARGET FOR TONIGHT: _____ hrs ☐

STRICT LIGHTS OUT TIME FOR TONIGHT: _____ : _____ ☐

OPENING UP ABOUT MY DAY:

_____

_____

_____

MY EVENING ROUTINE FOR TONIGHT:

1. _____ ☐
2. _____ ☐
3. _____ ☐
4. _____ ☐
5. _____ ☐

WHERE DO I WANT TO VISIT IN MY DREAMS TONIGHT?

_____

_____

SLEEP EXERCISE TO TRY TONIGHT (OPTIONAL):

WHEN READY FOR SLEEP, IMAGINE THE LIGHTS BEING SWITCHED OFF IN A LARGE BUILDING AT NIGHT. IMAGINE "SWITCHING OFF THE LIGHTS" FOR EACH PART OF YOUR BODY.

Day 17: **Pro-Tip**

<u>*A natural bedtime sleep remedy.*</u>

Although it's recommended that you don't eat too close to bedtime, there's a special remedy that you can drink before bed. It might not be the tastiest beverage, but many people swear by the benefits. This sleep remedy drink consists of hot water, honey, and apple cider vinegar (ACV)

What's so great about this drink? Honey and ACV both bring several benefits to the table. ACV is packed with vitamins and minerals that relieve symptoms of insomnia and help you to relax. It also controls your blood sugar, prevents and relieves nasal congestion, and prevents restlessness.

Honey promotes the production of melatonin. It also contains important vitamins and minerals, like calcium, B complex, and magnesium to promote muscle and full-body relaxation.

Here's how you make this super simple sleep remedy:

- Heat 8 ounces of water
- Stir in 2 tablespoons of ACV
- Add 1 tablespoon of honey (or more depending on your preference) to counteract the taste of ACV

"Sleep is the golden chain that ties health and our bodies together."
- Thomas Dekker

DATE _____

Completed?

SLEEP TARGET FOR TONIGHT: _____ hrs ☐

STRICT LIGHTS OUT TIME FOR TONIGHT: _____ : _____ ☐

OPENING UP ABOUT MY DAY:

_____
_____
_____

MY EVENING ROUTINE FOR TONIGHT:

1. _____ ☐
2. _____ ☐
3. _____ ☐
4. _____ ☐
5. _____ ☐

(Think: What headspace would be most beneficial for you to wake up in tomorrow?)

WHAT DO I WANT TO TELL MYSELF FIRST THING WHEN I WAKE UP TOMORROW?

_____
_____

SLEEP EXERCISE TO TRY TONIGHT (OPTIONAL):

WHEN YOU'RE READY TO SLEEP, CLOSE YOUR EYES AND COUNT SLOWLY. VISUALIZE EACH NUMBER BEING WRITTEN OR FORMED UNTIL YOU DRIFT TO SLEEP.

Day 18: **Favorite Resources**

Challenge: Try activating your vagus nerve.

The vagus nerve is the longest nerve in the body, connecting the brain to many important organs throughout the body, including the gut, heart, and lungs. The vagus nerve plays a massive role in your nervous system. It can help you move from a state of "fight-or-flight" to a resting state that relaxes your system by activating the parasympathetic nervous system.

If you want to relax your stress, tension, and anxiety, activating your vagus nerve can work wonders. Some ways to activate your vagus nerve include:

- Cold temperatures
- Singing or humming
- Probiotics for digestive health
- Meditation and breath work
- Massages
- Exercising
- Socializing
- Laughing

Another great way to stimulate your vagus nerve easily from home is to find a soft ball or a foam roller. Place it on the floor and place your abdominal area on the ball.

Spend 10 minutes lying on the ball or foam roller. Focus on your breathing. Since the vagus nerve is connected to the nervous system, don't be alarmed if you start feeling strong emotions. It's normal and natural, and it will pass. After your 10 minutes are up, you should feel less anxiety and stress, and ready to relax.

"Sleep is the best meditation." - Dalai Lama

DATE _____

Completed?

SLEEP TARGET FOR TONIGHT: _____ hrs ☐

STRICT LIGHTS OUT TIME FOR TONIGHT: _____ : _____ ☐

OPENING UP ABOUT MY DAY:

_____
_____
_____

MY EVENING ROUTINE FOR TONIGHT:

(How are you preparing for a restful evening?)

1. _____ ☐
2. _____ ☐
3. _____ ☐
4. _____ ☐
5. _____ ☐

WHAT OBSTACLES DO I FORESEE GETTING IN THE WAY OF HAVING A GREAT NIGHT'S SLEEP TONIGHT? (THINK: WHAT DO I NEED TO <u>AVOID</u> DOING?)

(What bad habits am I trying to get rid of?)

_____
_____

SLEEP EXERCISE TO TRY TONIGHT (OPTIONAL):

START PLAYING OUT A RANDOM SCENARIO IN YOUR HEAD. IT DOESN'T HAVE TO BE REALISTIC OR LOGICAL. KEEP GOING WITH YOUR STORY UNTIL YOUR BRAIN CONFUSES IT WITH DREAMING AND YOU FALL ASLEEP.

Day 19: **Pro-Tip**

Take advantage of your sleep window.

Your nervous system gives you a window of opportunity to fall asleep, which we often ignore or miss entirely.

Think of it like this: Have you ever felt extremely hungry for a while, but you didn't eat anything and the hungry feeling went away? The same thing can happen with sleep.

These sleep windows can make you feel super tired and so very ready for bed. But if you don't take advantage of them, your brain tells your body that it's time to rev back up. This is often the culprit behind someone getting a "second wind" and suddenly having a spike in energy.

When your body signals that it's ready for bed, acknowledge it and try to take advantage whenever possible.

Your sleep window occurs for a reason: Your body is trying to tell you what it needs, which is sleep! It gives you a perfect time, so don't let it pass you by.

"Never waste any time you can spend sleeping." - Frank H. Knight

DATE

X

Completed?

🛏️ SLEEP TARGET FOR TONIGHT: _____ hrs ☐

💡 STRICT LIGHTS OUT TIME FOR TONIGHT: _____ : _____ ☐

✏️ **OPENING UP ABOUT MY DAY:**

_____

_____

_____

🌙 **MY EVENING ROUTINE FOR TONIGHT:**

1. _____ ☐
2. _____ ☐
3. _____ ☐
4. _____ ☐
5. _____ ☐

💔 **HOW DID I POSITIVELY IMPACT SOMEONE ELSE TODAY?**

_____

_____

🛌 **SLEEP EXERCISE TO TRY TONIGHT** (OPTIONAL):

TUNE IN TO YOUR OWN HEARTBEAT. NEXT, PICK ANY LETTER IN THE ALPHABET. EVERY 8 HEARTBEATS, THINK OF A WORD THAT STARTS WITH THE LETTER YOU CHOSE.

Day 20: **Pro-Tip**

The power of "power naps."

The benefits of naps don't stop after your childhood years! As a matter of fact, the desire for a mid-afternoon nap is genetically hardwired into every person - no matter your age, geographical location, or cultural practice. Besides, who wouldn't enjoy a good excuse to nap?

While the option to nap isn't available to everyone, it's great to take advantage of nap opportunities whenever you feel like you really need it. Studies have proven that the refreshment from naps offers a stunning 20% learning and memory advantage compared to staying awake all day. It can also reverse some negative effects of sleep deprivation.

One awesome trick for getting a massive energy boost from your nap is called a nap-a-latte, created by sleep expert Dr. Michael Breus. For a nap-a-latte, start by getting a 6-8 ounce cup of coffee and drink it as quickly as possible. Follow that with a 25 minute nap. The combination of caffeine and sleep really amps up your alertness and energy levels.

You can also benefit from taking 15-20 minute naps 1-2 times during the day whenever possible if you prefer to avoid coffee or caffeine.

Avoid napping past 3 P.M., if not sooner, depending on how early your bedtime is. Sleeping too late in the afternoon can work against you by making it harder to fall asleep when it's finally bedtime.

"I count it as a certainty that in paradise, everyone naps."
- Tom Hodgkinson

DATE

Completed?

SLEEP TARGET FOR TONIGHT: _____ hrs ☐

STRICT LIGHTS OUT TIME FOR TONIGHT: _____ : _____ ☐

OPENING UP ABOUT MY DAY:

_____

_____

_____

MY EVENING ROUTINE FOR TONIGHT:

1. _____ ☐
2. _____ ☐
3. _____ ☐
4. _____ ☐
5. _____ ☐

WHY IS SLEEPING WELL TONIGHT SO IMPORTANT FOR MY DAY TOMORROW?

(Think: Why did you buy this journal in the first place?)

_____

_____

SLEEP EXERCISE TO TRY TONIGHT (OPTIONAL):

FORCE YOURSELF TO YAWN EVERY 20 SECONDS OR SO. AFTER A FEW YAWNS, YOUR BRAIN MIGHT GET TRICKED INTO FEELING SLEEPY.

Day 21: **Food For Thought**

<u>**Supplements for sleep.**</u>

Taking supplements in the evening to promote sleep can be extremely helpful in some situations. Ideally, supplementation should only be considered after trying everything else, and only if the other options didn't work for you.

Always consult your doctor when starting any supplements. Choose supplement brands carefully. Supplements aren't required to pass the same FDA regulations as foods and pharmaceuticals, so poor production quality can pose a huge problem.

The most common (and generally considered the safest) supplement options include:

- **Melatonin.** Melatonin should only be as a temporary solution for circadian rhythm disruptions (like "jet lag").
- **Valerian root.** If depression and anxiety frequently disrupt your sleep or diminish your sleep quality, supplementing with valerian root may be helpful.
- **Magnesium.** Magnesium deficiency has potential links to insomnia and poor sleep quality. Supplementing with magnesium can help you relax and regulate your circadian rhythm.
- **Glycine.** A study done on glycine supplements showed that those who took it felt less fatigued, more lively, and more clear-headed. It also helped participants fall asleep faster.

"Sleep is life's nurse, sent from heaven to create us anew day by day."
- Charles Reade

DATE

Completed?

SLEEP TARGET FOR TONIGHT: _____ hrs ☐

STRICT LIGHTS OUT TIME FOR TONIGHT: _____ : _____ ☐

OPENING UP ABOUT MY DAY:

_____
_____
_____

(Speak to yourself as if you were your own best friend!)

MY EVENING ROUTINE FOR TONIGHT:

1. _____ ☐
2. _____ ☐
3. _____ ☐
4. _____ ☐
5. _____ ☐

WHAT IS SOMETHING I DO DURING THE DAY THAT AFFECTS MY EVENING ROUTINE/SLEEP QUALITY? HOW CAN I CHANGE IT?

_____
_____

(Pay attention to how every action creates a chain effect.)

SLEEP EXERCISE TO TRY TONIGHT (OPTIONAL):

RELAX YOUR NECK, CHIN, JAW, AND TONGUE. LET YOUR TONGUE HANG FREE AND IMAGINE A WEIGHT PULLING YOUR CHIN DOWN TO RELEASE THE TENSION.

~~PHASE 2:~~
DESTROYED.

Phase 2 Recap: Days 8-21

1. What have you realized to be the most important elements for you to stick to a healthy sleep schedule?

_____

_____

2. What pre-bedtime sleep habits should you be doing consistently?

_____

_____

3. What are some new sleep strategies you want to experiment with?

_____

_____

4. How has your new sleep routine affected your life?

_____

_____

5. What impact would it have on your life if you stopped practicing this habit?

_____

_____

PHASE 3:
DAYS 22-66+

  **Phase 3**

~~Days 01-07~~ ~~Days 08-21~~ **Days 22-66+**
~~Hell Week.~~ ~~Staying Consistent.~~ **Rewiring Your Brain.**

Phase 3: Hardwiring - Retaining Interest in Your Personal Improvement

Congratulations, you've made it to Phase 3. You've shown serious commitment to the incredible future you envision for yourself.

This is a great phase to explore how to make the most out of this habit for you, personally. Most people use this phase to experiment with different evening routines, relaxation techniques, hours of sleep, etc. to tweak what works for them.

It's easy to take the benefits you're feeling for granted — it's extremely easy to fall off the wagon, especially in this phase.

Keep going strong until your new, healthy sleep schedule is engrained in your DNA.

This means pushing through to stick with your commitments on your best days, your worst days, and especially the days where you just don't feel like it (those are the *most important*).

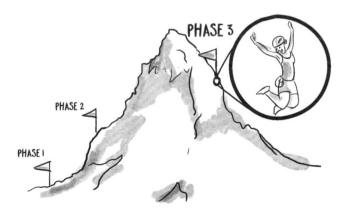

Commit.

I am INCREDIBLE.

*I've come a long way,
but the road doesn't end here.*

It's time to ingrain this habit in me forever.

*I will see this
huge challenge all the way through.*

*Mastering this habit is only the
beginning of my perpetual growth.*

_____

Nothing will stop me now.

_____   _____
Signature   Date

Phase 2 Medal Earned!

Day 22: **Pro-Tip**

<u>Black out your room.</u>

Having blackout curtains in your room is the best way to prevent any sleep and circadian rhythm disruptions caused by light.

When it's time to wind down in the evening, not even an eye mask can prevent the effects of light seeping through. Your skin, much like your eyes, has receptors that detect and take in light. So, even with your eyes covered, light can still affect your sleep!

- Try blackout curtains
- Dim or remove digital alarm clock displays
- Leave nightlights and TVs off

"Your future depends on your dreams, so go to sleep." - Mesut Barazany

DATE _____

Completed?

🛏️ SLEEP TARGET FOR TONIGHT: _____ hrs ☐

💡 STRICT LIGHTS OUT TIME FOR TONIGHT: _____ : _____ ☐

✏️ **OPENING UP ABOUT MY DAY:**

_____
_____
_____

☁️ **MY EVENING ROUTINE FOR TONIGHT:**

1. _____ ☐
2. _____ ☐
3. _____ ☐
4. _____ ☐
5. _____ ☐

💔 **WHAT AM I REALLY HAPPY ABOUT IN MY LIFE?**

(Focus on the positive. What's going incredibly well?)

_____
_____

🛌 **SLEEP EXERCISE TO TRY TONIGHT** (OPTIONAL):

THINK OF AN OBJECT OR WORD. CONTINUE THE STREAM OF THOUGHT BY FOLLOWING IT WITH THE NEXT WORD OR OBJECT THAT COMES TO MIND.

Day 23: **Food For Thought**

Reflect on the impact.

There will be plenty of times throughout this journey where you find yourself tempted to break away from your evening routine and good habits.

When this happens, try to reflect on the impact that your lack of sleep could have during the day after. Consider how it might impact you both physically and mentally.

Reflect on your 'why.' Remember why you chose to make these positive changes and think about how far you have come already.

If the temptation has to do with something like *YouTube*, social media, or video games, remind yourself that those things will still be there tomorrow. However, lost sleep is much harder to regain.

It's inevitable that you'll have nights of poor sleep. You might falter and break away from your evening routine. When faced with those situations, don't fret on them. Instead, create a battle plan for getting back on track and tackling these sleep habits with a renewed motivation and drive.

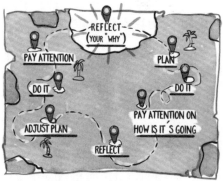

"Happiness consists of getting enough sleep. Just that, nothing more."
- Robert A. Heinlein

_____
DATE

Completed?

SLEEP TARGET FOR TONIGHT: _____ hrs ☐

STRICT LIGHTS OUT TIME FOR TONIGHT: _____ : _____ ☐

OPENING UP ABOUT MY DAY:

_____
_____
_____

MY EVENING ROUTINE FOR TONIGHT:

(How does each activity in your routine impact your evenings and sleep?)

1. _____ ☐
2. _____ ☐
3. _____ ☐
4. _____ ☐
5. _____ ☐

WHAT DO I NEED TO CHANGE IN REGARDS TO MY HABITS WITH SOCIAL APPS / GAMING / ENTERTAINMENT TO IMPROVE MY SLEEP?

_____
_____

SLEEP EXERCISE TO TRY TONIGHT (OPTIONAL):

LISTEN TO AN AUDIOBOOK WITH CALM, SOOTHING NARRATIONS TO HELP YOU DRIFT OFF.

Day 24: **Affirmations**

Calming your mind.

1. Find a quiet area where you can do this in private so you can be at ease. If you can't find a private space, say this in your head.
2. Think of a time when you felt absolutely relaxed, calm, and pleasant.
3. As you say the following words, imagine yourself in a place that makes you feel incredibly at ease.

I am breathing slowly and deeply. I am letting go and clearing my head of worries and racing thoughts. I am calm and sleepy. I am grateful, I am loved, and I have everything I need. I will get great sleep and greet the new day refreshed and ready.

Repeat this **one more time**.

"The best bridge between despair and hope is a good night's sleep."
- E. Joseph Crossman

_____
DATE

Completed?

SLEEP TARGET FOR TONIGHT: _____ hrs ☐

STRICT LIGHTS OUT TIME FOR TONIGHT: _____ : _____ ☐

OPENING UP ABOUT MY DAY:

_____
_____
_____

MY EVENING ROUTINE FOR TONIGHT:

1. _____ ☐
2. _____ ☐
3. _____ ☐
4. _____ ☐
5. _____ ☐

HOW DOES MY QUALITY OF SLEEP AFFECT MY MOOD? DOES THIS HAVE ANY SNOWBALL EFFECTS ON MY DAY I SHOULD BE MINDFUL OF?

_____
_____

(Consider how your daily energy levels impact your life.)

SLEEP EXERCISE TO TRY TONIGHT (OPTIONAL):

USE LAVENDER-SCENTED OILS, SPRAYS, LOTIONS, OR CANDLES FOR SOME SLEEP-INDUCING AROMATHERAPY.

Day 25: **Pro-Tip**

<u>Keep your mattress cool.</u>

There are few joys in life as wonderful as the feeling of turning the pillow over and feeling the cold on the other side pillow, right!?

Since cooling your core temperature is such an important factor in triggering sleep, keeping a cool mattress is a great way to promote deeper sleep.

There are many things you can do to help keep your mattress or sleeping area cool at night, including:

- A cooling pad to lie on
- Cooling units that blow cold air under the covers
- Pillows with good air flow
- An air conditioner unit near the bed
- Keep your ceiling fan turned on the highest speed

Some special mattresses also come with settings that allow you to set the temperature for your side of the bed. These especially come in handy if you share a bed with someone who has a different temperature preference.

"Discover the great ideas that lie inside you by discovering the power of sleep." - Arianna Huffington

DATE _____

Completed?

SLEEP TARGET FOR TONIGHT: _____ hrs ☐

STRICT LIGHTS OUT TIME FOR TONIGHT: _____ : _____ ☐

OPENING UP ABOUT MY DAY:

_____
_____
_____

MY EVENING ROUTINE FOR TONIGHT:

1. _____ ☐
2. _____ ☐
3. _____ ☐
4. _____ ☐
5. _____ ☐

WHAT EXTRA PREP-WORK CAN I DO TONIGHT THAT WOULD IMPROVE MY DAY TOMORROW?

_____
_____

SLEEP EXERCISE TO TRY TONIGHT (OPTIONAL):

IF YOU FEEL FRUSTRATED ABOUT NOT BEING ABLE TO SLEEP, PRACTICE DEEP BREATHING AND REPEAT TO YOURSELF, "MY BODY IS RESTING, AND REST IS PRODUCTIVE. SLEEP WILL COME TO ME, TOO."

Day 26: **Food For Thought**

The pros and cons of cellphones.

Rapidly improving cellphone technology has changed so many parts of our lives for the better - including our sleep habits - but it's not without flaws. Your phone can either be a super helpful sleep tool, or a sleep destroyer depending on how you use it.

Pros:

- Phones have alarms and apps to help you wake up
- They have several apps that are helpful for falling asleep
- Customizable settings allow you to block blue light and limit your usage
- Phones pair with wearable sleep & health trackers
- You can automate processes on your phone for bedtime and waking up

Cons:

- Studies prove that radiation from mobile phones delays sleep onset and interrupts sleep cycles
- That radiation wrecks your ability to enter deep sleep
- Phones are extremely distracting and can keep you awake
- Blue light from phone screens mess with your ability to fall asleep

The goal is to maximize the pros, and minimize the cons of cellphones when it comes to your sleep. Probably wise advice for the rest of your life too!

"*Sleep might be the most important aspect of building a great business, and having a high-performing body.*" - *Lewis Howes*

DATE _____

Completed?

SLEEP TARGET FOR TONIGHT: _____ hrs ☐

STRICT LIGHTS OUT TIME FOR TONIGHT: _____ : _____ ☐

OPENING UP ABOUT MY DAY:

_____

_____

_____

MY EVENING ROUTINE FOR TONIGHT:

1. _____ ☐
2. _____ ☐
3. _____ ☐
4. _____ ☐
5. _____ ☐

WHAT'S SOMETHING ON THE BACK OF MY MIND THAT'S STRESSING ME OUT AND WHAT CAN I DO TO ADDRESS IT TOMORROW?

(Can journaling help? Brainstorming solutions? What specific action will help resolve the issue?)

_____

_____

SLEEP EXERCISE TO TRY TONIGHT (OPTIONAL):

TRY CRANKING DOWN THE TEMPERATURE AND WEARING A PAIR OF COMFORTABLE, WARM SOCKS TO BED TO KEEP A COOLER CORE TEMPERATURE, BUT WARM FEET.

Day 27: **Pro-Tip**

Light can throw off your sleep.

Thousands of years of evolutionary fine-tuning led humans to follow patterns of light and darkness to coordinate our sleep and waking schedule. So you can imagine how big of a role light plays when it comes to regulating our circadian rhythm.

Sunlight is incredibly powerful in signaling your body that it's time to be awake and ready to go. Sunlight exposure is beneficial at any time of day, whether indoors or outdoors. However, your body is naturally more responsive to sunlight between 6 A.M. to 8:30 A.M., and direct sunlight outdoors is more beneficial than indirect sunlight.

Sunlight isn't the only form of light that has an impact. When artificial lighting was invented, our bodies had to acclimate to lighting that essentially varied the length of our days.

When it gets dark outside, artificial lighting tells our body that it's not bedtime yet. It affects our ability to get good-quality sleep without disruption or disorder. With our body clocks being thrown out of order by artificial light, sleep quality dwindles.

Early morning exposure to direct sunlight for 15-30 minutes is a great first step in regulating your circadian rhythm. As it gets closer to bedtime, progressively dimming or turning off artificial light in your house helps your body realize that it's time to prepare for sleep.

"It appears that every man's insomnia is as different from his neighbor's as are their daytime hopes and aspirations." - F. Scott Fitzgerald

DATE _____

Completed?

🛏️ SLEEP TARGET FOR TONIGHT: _____ hrs ☐

💡 STRICT LIGHTS OUT TIME FOR TONIGHT: ____ : ____ ☐

✏️ **OPENING UP ABOUT MY DAY:**

_____
_____
_____

🌙 **MY EVENING ROUTINE FOR TONIGHT:**

1. _____ ☐
2. _____ ☐
3. _____ ☐
4. _____ ☐
5. _____ ☐

💔 **WHERE DO I WANT TO VISIT IN MY DREAMS TONIGHT?**

_____
_____

🛌 **SLEEP EXERCISE TO TRY TONIGHT** (OPTIONAL):

IF YOU DON'T ALREADY, TRY MAKING YOUR BED. EVEN IF YOU DON'T MAKE IT UNTIL ALMOST BEDTIME, YOU WILL FEEL THE DOPAMINE RUSH OF COMPLETING A TASK AND CLIMB INTO A PLEASANTLY MADE BED, FEELING ACCOMPLISHED.

Day 28: **Pro-Tip**

<u>Try a buckwheat pillow.</u>

Buckwheat pillows are extremely popular in Korea, and word of the benefits of buckwheat pillows started spreading to other countries. Now, buckwheat pillows are in the spotlight for the comfortability, help with sleep posture, and cooling effect they offer.

As an added bonus, buckwheat pillows are generally cheaper than the regular synthetic pillows we are used to.

Since buckwheat pillows contain actual buckwheat hulls, the pillows are super moldable for maximum comfort. The movement of the hulls allow easy air flow, keeping your pillow nice and cool.

If you prefer it even colder, you can remove the hulls from the pillow and store them in the fridge or freezer. When you place them back in the case, your pillow will feel chilled and relaxing.

The only downside to a buckwheat pillow is that it is proven to store allergens and endotoxins that can flare allergies and asthma.

Luckily, there's a fix for that. Hypoallergenic pillow covers are available, which you can use to zip your buckwheat pillow into, which helps to seal away the allergens and endotoxins.

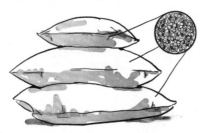

"That we are not much sicker and much madder than we are is due exclusively to that most blessed and blessing of all natural graces, sleep."
- Aldous Huxley

_____
DATE

Completed?

🛌 SLEEP TARGET FOR TONIGHT: _____ hrs ☐

💡 STRICT LIGHTS OUT TIME FOR TONIGHT: _____ : _____ ☐

✏️ **OPENING UP ABOUT MY DAY:**

_____
_____
_____

🌙 **MY EVENING ROUTINE FOR TONIGHT:**

1. _____ ☐
2. _____ ☐
3. _____ ☐
4. _____ ☐
5. _____ ☐

(Who do you want to be one year from now? What would that person tell you tomorrow morning?)

🔄 **WHAT DO I WANT TO TELL MYSELF FIRST THING WHEN I WAKE UP TOMORROW?**

_____
_____

🛏️ **SLEEP EXERCISE TO TRY TONIGHT** (OPTIONAL):

FAKE IT 'TIL YOU MAKE IT: THINK ABOUT HOW YOUR BODY AND MIND FEELS WHEN YOU ARE EXHAUSTED AND SLEEPY. MEDITATE ON IT AND IMAGINE YOUR BODY FEELING THAT WAY UNTIL IT FEELS AND BECOMES REAL.

Day 29: **Affirmations**

Inhale, exhale.

1. Find a quiet area where you can do this in private so you can be at ease. If you can't find a private space, say this in your head.
2. Think of a time when you felt absolutely relaxed, calm, and pleasant.
3. As you say the following words, imagine yourself in a place that makes you feel incredibly at ease.

Tonight, I choose peace; peace is in my soul. I choose to see with refreshed eyes. I inhale peace, and I exhale release. With each inhale, I gain wholesome energy. I inhale with mindfulness to the areas that need released. As I exhale, I release all tension and worry. Peace trickles in with each breath. Sleep now comes easier to me.

Repeat this **one more time.**

"We are such stuff as dreams are made on." - William Shakespeare

DATE _____

Completed?

SLEEP TARGET FOR TONIGHT: _____ hrs ☐

STRICT LIGHTS OUT TIME FOR TONIGHT: _____ : _____ ☐

OPENING UP ABOUT MY DAY:

_____

_____

_____

MY EVENING ROUTINE FOR TONIGHT:

1. _____ ☐
2. _____ ☐
3. _____ ☐
4. _____ ☐
5. _____ ☐

WHAT OBSTACLES DO I FORESEE GETTING IN THE WAY OF HAVING A GREAT NIGHT'S SLEEP TONIGHT? (THINK: WHAT DO I NEED TO <u>AVOID</u> DOING?)

_____

_____

SLEEP EXERCISE TO TRY TONIGHT (OPTIONAL):

IF YOU CAN'T SLEEP AFTER 20 MINUTES OF BEING IN BED, GET UP. TURN ON THE DIMMEST LIGHT YOU NEED AND FIND SOMETHING RELAXING TO DO (PREFERABLY SCREEN-FREE) LIKE READING, WRITING, DRINKING HOT HERBAL TEAS, ETC.

Day 30: **Pro-Tip**

<u>*Handling social "jet lag."*</u>

It's understandable and inevitable that your social life and your evening routine will sometimes clash. You might end up torn between sticking to your routine or attending social gatherings. What it comes down to is balance and personal preference.

If you want to go to an event and you're enjoying it, don't feel guilty about it. Having fun and keeping up with a healthy social rhythm is super important, too!

Bear in mind that you might experience "social jet lag," which is the groggy, brain-fog symptoms that happen when your social schedule doesn't align with your sleep schedule.

When it comes to balancing your social life, it takes a lot of experimenting and figuring out what works best for you. The key is maintaining as much consistency as possible, especially within a range. When you do have events or social gatherings that keep you up, get back on track the very next day!

"There is a time for many words, and there is also a time for sleep."
Homer

DATE _____

Completed?

🛏️ SLEEP TARGET FOR TONIGHT: _____ hrs ☐

💡 STRICT LIGHTS OUT TIME FOR TONIGHT: _____ : _____ ☐

✏️ **OPENING UP ABOUT MY DAY:**

_____

_____

_____

☁️ **MY EVENING ROUTINE FOR TONIGHT:**

1. _____ ☐
2. _____ ☐
3. _____ ☐
4. _____ ☐
5. _____ ☐

💔 **HOW DID I POSITIVELY IMPACT SOMEONE ELSE TODAY?**

_____

_____

🛌 **SLEEP EXERCISE TO TRY TONIGHT** (OPTIONAL):

AS YOU'RE TRYING TO FALL ASLEEP, TELL YOURSELF THAT YOUR ALARM WILL BE GOING OFF IN 5 MINUTES AND THAT YOU REALLY WANT AND NEED THAT LAST 5 MINUTES OF SLEEP. THIS TRICKS YOUR BRAIN INTO SLEEPINESS.

(Every small act of kindness starts a snowball effect of positivity that spreads through dozens, hundreds, or thousands of people.)

Day 31: **Pro-Tip**

<u>*Wearable sleep trackers.*</u>
Note: we have no affiliation with these companies or products, we just think they are great tools.

One amazing technology advancement, especially for health, is wearable trackers. These usually come in the form of a watch or a ring. They connect to your phone or devices and allow you to keep track of several areas of your health.

Most wearable trackers can also track your sleep cycles, oxygen levels, and heart rate. Some of the best wearable trackers for sleep include:

- <u>**Fitbit**</u>, which comes in the form of a watch. A Fitbit closely monitors your heart rate, how many steps you take, and your sleep cycles.
- <u>**Apple Watch**</u> doesn't directly track your sleep, but pairing it with sleep tracking apps on your phone or device allows it to use information from its sensors to analyze your sleep.
- <u>**Samsung Gear Watches**</u> have recently had a software upgrade that allows it to track your sleep and even monitor your REM sleep patterns.
- <u>**Oura Ring**</u> is a unique ring-wearable tracker jam-packed with different sensors for in-depth tracking. It focuses on your sleep and sleep readiness. It provides you with a score and tells you what factors need more of your attention to improve.
- <u>**Garmin Vivosmart**</u> is thinner and appears more like a bracelet, but don't let the size fool you. It's still full of sensors that provide valuable information about your health and sleep.

DATE _____

Completed?

SLEEP TARGET FOR TONIGHT: _____ hrs ☐

STRICT LIGHTS OUT TIME FOR TONIGHT: _____ : _____ ☐

OPENING UP ABOUT MY DAY:

_____
_____
_____

MY EVENING ROUTINE FOR TONIGHT:

1. _____ ☐
2. _____ ☐
3. _____ ☐
4. _____ ☐
5. _____ ☐

WHY IS SLEEPING WELL TONIGHT SO IMPORTANT FOR MY DAY TOMORROW?

_____
_____

(Think larger. How does getting good sleep tonight lead to getting good sleep tomorrow night, and how does building that HABIT impact your LIFE?)

SLEEP EXERCISE TO TRY TONIGHT (OPTIONAL):

TAKE A HOT BATH AROUND 90 MINUTES BEFORE BEDTIME. STUDIES SHOW THAT THIS IS THE OPTIMAL TIME FRAME FOR THE MOST BENEFIT FROM YOUR TUB TIME.

Day 32: **Pro-Tip**

<u>Avoid alcohol and certain medications before bed.</u>

Alcohol in the evening may make you feel tired, but the higher your blood-alcohol content rises, the longer it takes to fall asleep. It suppresses REM sleep and dehydrates your body, leading to awful sleep quality.

A good rule of thumb when you drink is to try waiting 1 hour for each alcoholic drink before lying down for bed. It can also be helpful to drink 1 glass of water per beverage to combat dehydration.

When it comes to prescribed medications, it's important to understand that sedation isn't the same thing as sleep. Sedatives make you unconscious, but they don't allow you to get the deep sleep you need to refresh and revitalize each night. For this reason, sleeping pills are best saved as a last resort option, when possible.

Other medications that disrupt your sleep include some commonly prescribed blood pressure medications, blood thinners, and asthma medications. Talking to your doctor about your medications and how they might affect your sleep can get you on the right track.

"A good laugh and a long sleep are the best cures in the doctor's book"
- Irish Proverb

DATE _____

Completed?

SLEEP TARGET FOR TONIGHT: _____ hrs ☐

STRICT LIGHTS OUT TIME FOR TONIGHT: _____ : _____ ☐

✏ OPENING UP ABOUT MY DAY:

_____

_____

_____

🌙 MY EVENING ROUTINE FOR TONIGHT:

1. _____ ☐
2. _____ ☐
3. _____ ☐
4. _____ ☐
5. _____ ☐

💤 WHAT IS SOMETHING I DO DURING THE DAY THAT AFFECTS MY EVENING ROUTINE/SLEEP QUALITY? HOW CAN I CHANGE IT?

_____

_____

🛏 SLEEP EXERCISE TO TRY TONIGHT (OPTIONAL):

AT DINNER, TRY EATING SOMETHING HIGH IN VITAMIN D AND OMEGA 3 FATTY ACIDS (IDEALLY, OILY FISH LIKE TUNA OR SALMON). THESE HELP PROMOTE BETTER SLEEP.

Day 33: **Favorite Resources**

Recommended app: SleepScore.

Note: we have no affiliation with SleepScore. We just love their product.

SleepScore comes highly recommended for maintaining sleep accountability. It allows you to set and track a variety of sleep goals, and it tracks and analyzes your sleep.

Using your microphone, *SleepScore* is able to assess your breathing, movement, and brief awakenings throughout the entire night.

By combining all the collected information and presenting it as a score, it allows you to better figure out where you stand on sleep quality. It also provides charts that are easy to read and understand. It puts a ton of sleep analytics at your disposal without making it overly complicated.

SleepScore does offer a paid version, but the free version still provides a ton of great features, including a special alarm clock.

The *SleepScore* app is available for both Android and iOS devices!

"Sleeplessness is a desert without vegetation or inhabitants."
- Jessamyn West

DATE _____

Completed?

🛏️ SLEEP TARGET FOR TONIGHT: _____ hrs ☐

💡 STRICT LIGHTS OUT TIME FOR TONIGHT: _____ : _____ ☐

✏️ **OPENING UP ABOUT MY DAY:**

_____
_____
_____

🌙 **MY EVENING ROUTINE FOR TONIGHT:**

1. _____ ☐
2. _____ ☐
3. _____ ☐
4. _____ ☐
5. _____ ☐

💔 **WHAT AM I REALLY HAPPY ABOUT IN MY LIFE?**

_____
_____

🛌 **SLEEP EXERCISE TO TRY TONIGHT** (OPTIONAL):

IF YOU FEEL TEMPTED TO SNEAK A PEEK AT YOUR PHONE WHEN YOU CAN'T FALL ASLEEP, MOVE YOUR PHONE SOMEWHERE OUT OF REACH.

Day 34: **Daily Challenge**

Challenge: Practice good sleep posture.

Sleep posture is an important aspect of good-quality sleep that is largely ignored. Without good sleep posture, you wake up with joint pain, stiffness, and sleepiness from an uncomfortable night of sleep.

According to *Johns Hopkins Medicine*, the best sleep posture for you depends on what conditions you may be dealing with.

On average, the best sleep posture includes:

- Having your neck aligned with your spine
- Keeping your spine straight and aligned
- Bending your knees
- Aligning your heels with your shoulders

To learn more about better sleep posture, check out hopkinsmedicine.org for more. The website includes more details about how to sleep better if you struggle with heartburn, sleep apnea, and other conditions to help you get a night of pain-free sleep.

"But sleep - good sleep, and enough of it - this is a necessity without which you cannot have the exercise of use, nor the food."
- Edward Everett Hale

DATE _____

Completed?

🛏️ SLEEP TARGET FOR TONIGHT: _____ hrs ☐

💡 STRICT LIGHTS OUT TIME FOR TONIGHT: ____ : ____ ☐

✏️ **OPENING UP ABOUT MY DAY:**

_____

_____

_____

🌥️ **MY EVENING ROUTINE FOR TONIGHT:**

1. _____
2. _____
3. _____
4. _____
5. _____

(Try making each step an increasingly relaxing activity. Start with more active things, and move into more passive actions.)

💤 **WHAT DO I NEED TO CHANGE IN REGARDS TO MY HABITS WITH SOCIAL APPS / GAMING / ENTERTAINMENT TO IMPROVE MY SLEEP?**

_____

_____

🛌 **SLEEP EXERCISE TO TRY TONIGHT** (OPTIONAL):

WHILE LYING IN BED, DO SOME SUBTRACTING. START AT 1,000 AND COUNT BACKWARD BY 7S. FOR EXAMPLE: 1,000…993…986…ETC.

Day 35: **Pro-Tip**

<u>*Get your vitamin and mineral levels checked.*</u>

When you think about the factors that contribute to getting a great night of sleep, vitamins and minerals are likely the last thing that comes to mind.

Getting the right amount of vitamins and minerals is what your brain needs to produce and release the neurotransmitters that promote sleep in the evening. The most common deficiencies linked to insomnia, poor sleep, and daytime sleepiness include:

- Vitamin B12
- Vitamin D
- Iron
- Magnesium

A quick and easy blood test by a doctor or nutrition expert will tell you if you're missing out on any of these important vitamins and minerals.

If you have a deficiency, your doctor might suggest or prescribe supplements. Another great way to boost your levels is by adding foods into your diet that are rich in these nutrients.

Once you start getting the right nutrients, you'll be well on your way to great sleep!

"If you get tired, learn to rest, not to quit." - Banksy

DATE _____

Completed?

SLEEP TARGET FOR TONIGHT: _____ hrs ☐

STRICT LIGHTS OUT TIME FOR TONIGHT: _____ : _____ ☐

✎ OPENING UP ABOUT MY DAY:

_____
_____
_____

☾ MY EVENING ROUTINE FOR TONIGHT:

1. _____ ☐
2. _____ ☐
3. _____ ☐
4. _____ ☐
5. _____ ☐

💔 HOW DOES MY QUALITY OF SLEEP AFFECT MY MOOD? DOES THIS HAVE ANY SNOWBALL EFFECTS ON MY DAY I SHOULD BE MINDFUL OF?

_____
_____

🛏 SLEEP EXERCISE TO TRY TONIGHT (OPTIONAL):

WHEN YOU'RE TRYING TO FALL ASLEEP, CLOSE YOUR EYES AND VISUALIZE A COMFORTING PLACE YOU'VE LIVED OR VISITED. ROAM THE HALLS, CHECK OUT EACH ROOM, AND PICTURE ALL THE DETAILS. THIS HELPS DISTRACT YOUR MIND AND BRING COMFORT.

Day 36: **Pro-Tip**

<u>Do a "closing ritual" to separate your work day from your evening.</u>

Your evening ritual works best if you have drawn a clear line to separate your day from your night. Once it's time for your evening ritual to begin, your work day should be considered complete and closed.

At the designated time to begin your evening routine, find a ritual or way of telling yourself that it's time to put the events and obligations of the day behind you.

Imagine walking through the door at home and having everything from your day fall away as you cross the threshold. Make your home - or even just a certain spot in your home - a barrier that doesn't allow your day to cross it and invade your evening.

If work requires a uniform, badge, or briefcase, hang them up for the night (preferable somewhere mostly out of sight). If not, change into some comfortable clothes or pajamas. While doing so, remind yourself that you've done everything you can do, and that you are now free of your daytime responsibilities. If it helps you further separate from your work day, take a shower and visualize scrubbing away the obligations and stress of the day.

You may have a unique closing ritual that works best for you, so feel free to experiment with other methods.

By helping us keep the world in perspective, sleep gives us a chance to refocus on the essence of who we are." - Arianna Huffington

_____
DATE

Completed?

SLEEP TARGET FOR TONIGHT: _____ hrs ☐

STRICT LIGHTS OUT TIME FOR TONIGHT: _____ : _____ ☐

OPENING UP ABOUT MY DAY:

_____
_____
_____

MY EVENING ROUTINE FOR TONIGHT:

1. _____ ☐
2. _____ ☐
3. _____ ☐
4. _____ ☐
5. _____ ☐

(You NEVER regret front-loading something you were going to do later.)

WHAT EXTRA PREP-WORK CAN I DO TONIGHT THAT WOULD IMPROVE MY DAY TOMORROW?

_____
_____

SLEEP EXERCISE TO TRY TONIGHT (OPTIONAL):

WHEN BEDTIME IS AN HOUR AWAY, DRINK A 16 OUNCE WATER BOTTLE TO HYDRATE BEFORE BED. THIS GIVES IT TIME TO HYDRATE YOUR SYSTEM AND USE THE RESTROOM.

Day 37: **Daily Challenge**

Challenge: Try the Wim Hof method.

Wim Hof is a Dutch athlete who is well-known for his ability to withstand extremely cold temperatures. Using a variety of meditations, practices, and breath work, Wim Hof's method and techniques are said to:

- Help improve your tolerance for cold temperatures
- Get better sleep and feel more energetic
- Improve your mental health and well-being
- Increase your willpower
- Regulate your autonomic nervous system, which plays a role in your ability to sleep well by increasing your heart rate variability.

Wim Hof's method can be really valuable for anyone that struggles with cold temperatures, willpower, mental health, and getting good sleep.

You can find Wim Hof's method at:

- Online at www.wimhofmethod.com
- The *Wim Hoff* mobile app for Android and iPhone
- Wim Hof's book *The Wim Hof Method*

"Each night, when I go to sleep, I die. And the next morning, when I wake up, I'm reborn." - Gandhi

DATE

Completed?

SLEEP TARGET FOR TONIGHT: _____ hrs ☐

STRICT LIGHTS OUT TIME FOR TONIGHT: _____ : _____ ☐

OPENING UP ABOUT MY DAY:

_____
_____
_____

MY EVENING ROUTINE FOR TONIGHT:

1. _____ ☐
2. _____ ☐
3. _____ ☐
4. _____ ☐
5. _____ ☐

WHAT'S SOMETHING ON THE BACK OF MY MIND THAT'S STRESSING ME OUT AND WHAT CAN I DO TO ADDRESS IT TOMORROW?

_____
_____

SLEEP EXERCISE TO TRY TONIGHT (OPTIONAL):

BEFORE BED, TRY FINISHING AN AVERAGE-SIZED CROSSWORD PUZZLE. NOT ONLY IS THIS GREAT FOR EXERCISING YOUR COGNITIVE FUNCTION, BUT IT TIRES YOUR BRAIN AND READIES IT FOR REST.

Day 38: **Pro-Tip**

Helpful phone features.

Using your phone in the evening isn't always bad, especially if you use the tools and apps available to relax and unwind in the evening. If you have an Android or Apple phone, try out these functions for winding down in the evening:

Bedtime Mode. For Android devices, this allows you to schedule and turn on "Do Not Disturb", which silences calls, texts, and notifications. On iOS devices, it also lets you set sleep goals in the Health app and even lock your phone after a certain time. (Note: This is found under the *Clock* app for iOS devices).

Wind Down Mode is great for customizing and automating an evening routine. You can set it to start soothing sounds, music, and meditation from other apps at a certain time. It also automatically turns on "Sleep Mode" and "Do Not Disturb." If your schedule changes, you can dismiss "Wind Down" that evening.

The Clock app lets you keep a calendar and schedule, adjust your sleep and wake times, and sends you reminders when it's time for bed. It also has the option to begin playing soothing sounds or music from other apps.

Screen time limits and Apple Screen Time allow you to be more aware and mindful of your screen time. These functions also let you set customizable daily limits on any app.

"Tired minds don't plan well. Sleep first, plan later." - Walter Reisch

DATE _____

Completed?

🛏️ SLEEP TARGET FOR TONIGHT: _____ hrs ☐

💡 STRICT LIGHTS OUT TIME FOR TONIGHT: _____ : _____ ☐

✏️ **OPENING UP ABOUT MY DAY:**

_____
_____
_____

🌙 **MY EVENING ROUTINE FOR TONIGHT:**

1. _____ ☐
2. _____ ☐
3. _____ ☐
4. _____ ☐
5. _____ ☐

💕 **WHERE DO I WANT TO VISIT IN MY DREAMS TONIGHT?**

_____
_____

🛌 **SLEEP EXERCISE TO TRY TONIGHT** (OPTIONAL):

IF YOU GET HUNGRY TOO CLOSE TO BEDTIME, DRINK A WARM GLASS OF MILK, WHETHER IT'S COW'S MILK OR DAIRY-FREE ALTERNATIVES. IT WILL FILL YOUR BELLY AND HELP YOU FEEL RELAXED.

Day 39: Pro-Tip

Sleep in relation to your diet.

Your sleep and diet influence each other. It's a cycle that can spin out of control quickly if either your diet or sleep is of poor quality.

If you've ever noticed that you feel hungry when you're very tired, there's a biological reason. When you're sleep deprived, the hormone that makes you hungry (ghrelin) increases. At the same time, the hormone that signals that you're full (leptin) decreases.

In this case, you feel more hungry because you're tired and your body wants energy, and on top of that, it takes more food to feel full. It can cause you to consume extra calories, especially carbs, sugars, and processed foods. Your body also mismanages where those calories should go.

When you achieve good, quality sleep, your body is better able to regulate your metabolism and appetite. It keeps a better balance of insulin and blood glucose. Good nutrition in addition to sleep allows a healthy gut microbiome to flourish, which is essential for good nutritional health and overall well-being.

"Early to bed and early to rise makes a man healthy, wealthy, and wise."
- Benjamin Franklin

DATE _____

Completed?

🛏️ SLEEP TARGET FOR TONIGHT: _____ hrs ☐

💡 STRICT LIGHTS OUT TIME FOR TONIGHT: _____ : _____ ☐

✏️ **OPENING UP ABOUT MY DAY:**

_____
_____
_____

🌙 **MY EVENING ROUTINE FOR TONIGHT:**

1. _____ ☐
2. _____ ☐
3. _____ ☐
4. _____ ☐
5. _____ ☐

↻ **WHAT DO I WANT TO TELL MYSELF FIRST THING WHEN I WAKE UP TOMORROW?**

_____
_____

🛌 **SLEEP EXERCISE TO TRY TONIGHT** (OPTIONAL):

IF YOU FEEL STRESSED OR ANXIOUS BEFORE BED, IMMERSE YOUR FACE IN ICY WATER FOR 30-45 SECONDS. YOUR NERVOUS SYSTEM WILL REFLEXIVELY LOWER YOUR HEART RATE AND BLOOD PRESSURE IN RESPONSE.

Day 40: **Daily Challenge**

Challenge: Implement a phone curfew.

A massively important tool for getting great sleep is having a phone curfew. Kicking back and putting away the screen for even 5, 15, or 30 minutes before bed can help your brain better recognize that it's time to wind down.

Blue light exposure aside, the stimulation from your phone in the form of information through social media, apps, and news sources is overload for a brain preparing to sleep.

Much of this information can overwhelm your brain or make you feel stressed and anxious about current events and even relationships. Of course, that means your sleep suffers the consequences of your stressed state.

Tonight, try implementing a phone curfew. Aim for a phone curfew of 10-20 minutes before bedtime. Use this time to relax and debrief from a long day of work, technology, and information overload. Eventually, try to work up to putting your phone aside for 60-90 minutes (or more!) before bed.

"Finish each day before you begin the next, and interpose a solid wall of sleep between the two. This you cannot do without temperance."
- Ralph Waldo Emerson

DATE _____

Completed?

🛏️ SLEEP TARGET FOR TONIGHT: _____ hrs ☐

💡 STRICT LIGHTS OUT TIME FOR TONIGHT: _____ : _____ ☐

✏️ **OPENING UP ABOUT MY DAY:**

_____
_____
_____

🌥️ **MY EVENING ROUTINE FOR TONIGHT:**

1. _____ ☐
2. _____ ☐
3. _____ ☐
4. _____ ☐
5. _____ ☐

💤 **WHAT OBSTACLES DO I FORESEE GETTING IN THE WAY OF HAVING A GREAT NIGHT'S SLEEP TONIGHT?** (THINK: WHAT DO I NEED TO <u>AVOID</u> DOING?)

_____
_____

🛏️ **SLEEP EXERCISE TO TRY TONIGHT** (OPTIONAL):

INDULGE IN A GLASS OF TART CHERRY JUICE 2 HOURS BEFORE LIGHTS-OUT. TART CHERRY JUICE IS RICH IN MELATONIN.

Day 41: **Pro-Tip**

<u>Try a light therapy lamp.</u>

Light therapy lamps are recommended for a multitude of medical conditions, which include sleep and circadian rhythm disorders.

Using the light therapy lamp throughout the day helps to regulate your circadian rhythm by exposing your body to light that is similar to sunlight. Once you turn it off and start limiting light exposure, your body gets the signal that it's time to relax.

These lamps emit a bright light while filtering out any harmful ultraviolet (UV) rays that come from sunlight. They usually use white lighting that simulates noonday sunlight, keeping your brain awake and alert throughout the day.

Most light therapy lamps have a simplistic, minimalistic design that fits perfectly on desks and other work surfaces. Many of them are portable in case you need to take your lamp with you.

As with any other habit, light therapy lamps require consistency to see any real results. If you keep up with your light therapy, you'll notice a big difference in your circadian rhythm and promote good sleep at the same time!

"Sleep deprivation is an illegal torture method outlawed by the Geneva Convention and international courts, but most of us do it to ourselves."
- Ryan Hurd

DATE _____

Completed?

☾ SLEEP TARGET FOR TONIGHT: _____ hrs ☐

💡 STRICT LIGHTS OUT TIME FOR TONIGHT: _____ : _____ ☐

✏️ **OPENING UP ABOUT MY DAY:**

_____
_____
_____

☁️ **MY EVENING ROUTINE FOR TONIGHT:**

1. _____ ☐
2. _____ ☐
3. _____ ☐
4. _____ ☐
5. _____ ☐

💔 **HOW DID I POSITIVELY IMPACT SOMEONE ELSE TODAY?**

_____
_____

🛏️ **SLEEP EXERCISE TO TRY TONIGHT** (OPTIONAL):

TRY TAKING A BREAK FROM SLEEP-DISRUPTING SCREENS AND BLUE LIGHT BY HAVING A CANDLE-LIT DINNER.

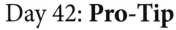

Day 42: **Pro-Tip**

<u>*Consider ditching your alarm.*</u>

Has your alarm ever scared you awake? Or maybe hearing an alarm clock just feels like an annoying way to start your day? That's because the loud, jarring noise from alarm clocks can trigger our "fight-or-flight" state.

Having alarm clocks suddenly pull you out of peaceful sleep can actually cause a blood pressure spike, an increased heart rate, and other effects due to the sudden shock to your nervous system.

For many people, once they find how many hours their body naturally needs, waking up naturally and without alarms is preferable. It allows a more gentle, calm, peaceful start to their morning. It allows the completion of all the necessary sleep cycles, allowing them to wake up refreshed and ready for their day.

It may take some time, training, and experimenting, but ditching your alarm clock can considerably improve your sleep quality. Consider giving it a try and assessing what difference it makes for your sleep and your mornings.

"A good night's sleep is always the best way to wake up and go to work."
- Chanel Iman

_____
DATE

(It's Day 42!!! That means you've been working really hard. Don't take for granted how this habit is impacting your life once it starts to feel normal!)

Completed?

SLEEP TARGET FOR TONIGHT: _____ hrs ☐

STRICT LIGHTS OUT TIME FOR TONIGHT: _____ : _____ ☐

OPENING UP ABOUT MY DAY:

_____
_____
_____

MY EVENING ROUTINE FOR TONIGHT:

1. _____ ☐
2. _____ ☐
3. _____ ☐
4. _____ ☐
5. _____ ☐

WHY IS SLEEPING WELL TONIGHT SO IMPORTANT FOR MY DAY TOMORROW?

_____
_____

SLEEP EXERCISE TO TRY TONIGHT (OPTIONAL):

BLOW BUBBLES BEFORE BED. IT MAY SOUND SILLY, BUT IT PROMOTES DEEP BREATHING AND ACTS AS A CALMING ACTIVITY.

Day 43: **Food For Thought**

Start a "worry" journal.

Anxiety is undoubtedly a destroyer of good sleep. It keeps your mind racing and doesn't allow you to rest, physically or mentally.

If you find yourself frequently dealing with anxiety or stress in the evening, consider writing in a worry journal. A worry journal allows you to dump all your anxious feelings onto the pages.

It helps you express your feelings, and sometimes even discover solutions. The goal is to reduce your anxieties and hush those racing thoughts.

After getting those anxieties off your chest, leave those worries in the journal. Those worries shouldn't cross the threshold into your sleep sanctuary.

Whatever is worrying you can wait until tomorrow. For now, you can't handle it very efficiently without a well-rested brain.

"The minute anyone's getting anxious I say, 'You must eat and you must sleep.' They're the two vital elements for a healthy life." - Francesca Annis

DATE

Completed?

SLEEP TARGET FOR TONIGHT: _____ hrs ☐

STRICT LIGHTS OUT TIME FOR TONIGHT: _____ : _____ ☐

OPENING UP ABOUT MY DAY:

_____
_____
_____

MY EVENING ROUTINE FOR TONIGHT:

1. _____ ☐
2. _____ ☐
3. _____ ☐
4. _____ ☐
5. _____ ☐

WHAT IS SOMETHING I DO DURING THE DAY THAT AFFECTS MY EVENING ROUTINE/SLEEP QUALITY? HOW CAN I CHANGE IT?

(If you pay close attention, you can continue to learn more about yourself through this question.)

_____
_____

SLEEP EXERCISE TO TRY TONIGHT (OPTIONAL):

WHILE TRYING TO FALL ASLEEP, CLOSE YOUR EYES. KEEPING THEM CLOSED, ROLL YOUR EYES AS IF YOU'RE DRAWING PICTURES ON THE INSIDE OF YOUR EYELIDS. USE THEM TO DRAW ANYTHING (LETTERS, NUMBERS, PICTURES, ETC).

Day 44: **Pro-Tip**

<u>*Let music soothe you to sleep.*</u>

Music is an amazing thing. It has the power to make us feel certain ways, it provokes emotion, and it even affects our brain.

Music can dramatically impact our sleep. Multiple studies have proven that calm, relaxing music helps you fall asleep easier and faster.

Not all music is equal when it comes to this. If you lie down to sleep while listening to a loud song that pumps you up, your brain definitely won't relax.

Classical music and other slow, soothing songs are the most effective. When songs have a rhythm of 60 beats per minute, something surprising happens. Your heart rate begins to tune itself to the rhythm of the song as you drift off to sleep.

Try listening to some of your favorite soothing songs or some ambient soundscapes designed specifically for sleep. Experiment with songs that have a 60 beats-per-minute rhythm in the evening and check out how it makes you feel and how it impacts your sleep.

"Even a soul submerged in sleep is hard at work and helps make something of the world." - Heraclitus

_____ DATE

Completed?

SLEEP TARGET FOR TONIGHT: _____ hrs ☐

STRICT LIGHTS OUT TIME FOR TONIGHT: _____ : _____ ☐

OPENING UP ABOUT MY DAY:

_____
_____
_____

MY EVENING ROUTINE FOR TONIGHT:

1. _____ ☐
2. _____ ☐
3. _____ ☐
4. _____ ☐
5. _____ ☐

WHAT AM I REALLY HAPPY ABOUT IN MY LIFE?

_____
_____

SLEEP EXERCISE TO TRY TONIGHT (OPTIONAL):

BEFORE BED, DE-CLUTTER YOUR ROOM AND REMOVE DISTRACTIONS. IF YOU HAVE BILLS OR PILES OF OTHER PAPERWORK, TAKE THEM OUT. THIS KEEPS YOUR ROOM FREE OF STRESS AND MESS.

Day 45: **Super Read**

"Why We Sleep" by Matthew Walker.

Matthew Walker's book, *Why We Sleep* offers an in-depth, knowledgeable exploration of the science behind sleep. Matthew Walker is a psychologist, sleep expert, and professor that has spent much of his career performing studies and learning about sleep.

In general, sleep is still considered a mystery. The evolution behind sleep and circadian rhythms, the scientific side of why we sleep and how things affect sleep, it's all here inside Matthew Walker's book.

Education and knowledge are the highest form of power. The more you understand your body and sleep, the more insights you have that can help improve your sleep habits and be more in control of your sleep habits.

The book explores so many topics that you wouldn't fathom could be related to sleep or affect how you sleep. It's an amazing book for anyone that's curious and wants to learn how to understand how their body works.

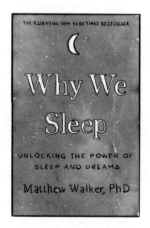

"Man is a genius when he is dreaming." - Akira Kurosawa

DATE _____

Completed?

SLEEP TARGET FOR TONIGHT: _____ hrs ☐

STRICT LIGHTS OUT TIME FOR TONIGHT: ____ : ____ ☐

OPENING UP ABOUT MY DAY:

_____

_____

_____

MY EVENING ROUTINE FOR TONIGHT:

1. _____ ☐
2. _____ ☐
3. _____ ☐
4. _____ ☐
5. _____ ☐

WHAT DO I NEED TO CHANGE IN REGARDS TO MY HABITS WITH SOCIAL APPS / GAMING / ENTERTAINMENT TO IMPROVE MY SLEEP?

_____

_____

SLEEP EXERCISE TO TRY TONIGHT (OPTIONAL):

TRY ALTERNATE NOSTRIL BREATHING FOR 5 MINUTES. PLUG YOUR RIGHT NOSTRIL AND INHALE THROUGH THE LEFT. THEN, PLUG YOUR LEFT NOSTRIL AND EXHALE THROUGH THE RIGHT. REPEAT, STARTING BY INHALING THROUGH THE RIGHT.

Day 46: **Pro-Tip**

Don't over-schedule yourself.

It is incredibly important to enter the night with time to unwind before actually going to sleep. Over-scheduling and over-working into the hours and minutes just before bed comes with undesirable consequences for your sleep.

Leave a block of your schedule open for your evening routine. Give yourself plenty of time to relax and prepare for bedtime.

Some relaxing activities to insert into your evening routine to help you unwind are:

- Reading
- Listening to music
- Taking a hot bath
- Turning off lights and using candlelight
- Lighting candles or incense with soothing scents
- Changing into super comfortable pajamas

Your schedule needs to be realistic and healthy, which means it needs to include your bedtime routine and a proper sleep schedule. Any other tasks on your schedule that can wait will likely benefit from you achieving a night of good rest, anyways!

"Sleep is not a waste of time. During sleep, a variety of biological processes take place that restore our bodies and minds."
- Nancy Foldvary-Schaefer

DATE _____

Completed?

SLEEP TARGET FOR TONIGHT: _____ hrs ☐

STRICT LIGHTS OUT TIME FOR TONIGHT: _____ : _____ ☐

OPENING UP ABOUT MY DAY:

_____
_____
_____

MY EVENING ROUTINE FOR TONIGHT:

1. _____ ☐
2. _____ ☐
3. _____ ☐
4. _____ ☐
5. _____ ☐

HOW DOES MY QUALITY OF SLEEP AFFECT MY MOOD? DOES THIS HAVE ANY SNOWBALL EFFECTS ON MY DAY I SHOULD BE MINDFUL OF?

(Mood largely determines perspective. Don't take for granted how important it is to your quality of life.)

_____
_____

SLEEP EXERCISE TO TRY TONIGHT (OPTIONAL):

GATHER SOME EXTRA PILLOWS AND SURROUND YOURSELF WITH PILLOWY SOFTNESS IN BED. YOU CAN ALSO PLACE THEM IN SPOTS THAT NEED MORE SUPPORT, SUCH AS BETWEEN YOUR KNEES OR AROUND ANY PAIN POINTS.

Day 47: **Pro-Tip**

Bring your pets to bed.

If you have pets, invite them to snuggle in your bed! Pets provide emotional support and promote relaxation. Interacting with your pet triggers oxytocin, which is the feel-good, happy hormone. Oxytocin helps you create a deep, therapeutic bond with your pets.

Even beyond just creating bonds, oxytocin has plenty of major benefits of its own. It creates a healthier environment in your body, helps your body heal, and promotes the growth of new cells. Who would have thought that snuggling your pets could be so beneficial?

If you worry that having your pet in bed will be a distraction, try training them to sleep in a certain area or provide them with their own pillow or small pet bed. Their close proximity is still enough to bring you comfort!

"Oh sleep! It is a gentle thing, beloved from pole to pole."
- Samuel Taylor Coleridge

DATE _____

Completed?

🛏️ SLEEP TARGET FOR TONIGHT: _____ hrs ☐

💡 STRICT LIGHTS OUT TIME FOR TONIGHT: _____ : _____ ☐

✏️ **OPENING UP ABOUT MY DAY:**

_____
_____
_____

🌙 **MY EVENING ROUTINE FOR TONIGHT:**

(What do you always say you want more of in your life but don't make time for?)

1. _____ ☐
2. _____ ☐
3. _____ ☐
4. _____ ☐
5. _____ ☐

🔄 **WHAT EXTRA PREP-WORK CAN I DO TONIGHT THAT WOULD IMPROVE MY DAY TOMORROW?**

_____
_____

🛌 **SLEEP EXERCISE TO TRY TONIGHT** (OPTIONAL):

BEFORE BED, TAKE A FEW MINUTES TO JOT DOWN A TO-DO LIST FOR TOMORROW. USE PEN/PENCIL AND PAPER. ONCE YOU HAVE IT WRITTEN OUT, YOUR MIND WILL BE CLEAR OF INTRUSIVE THOUGHTS ABOUT WHAT NEEDS TO BE DONE.

Day 48: **Daily Challenge**

Challenge: Practice gratitude before bed.

After a long day of work, errands, caring for others, and everything else life throws at us, it's easy to lose sight of what's really important.

We tend focus on what went wrong that day instead of what went right. This dwelling, stressing, and anxiety create massive obstacles that block the way to good sleep.

By practicing gratitude before going to bed, you settle your racing thoughts and break free from anxiety. By focusing on the parts of your life that you can be grateful for, you produce feel-good hormones and allow your mind to rest.

Tonight, try writing a list of what you're grateful for. Write at least 5 things, but feel free to write more than that! Think about everything that made you happy, made you smile, and made you feel good today and focus on those things.

Adopt a positive mindset that the upcoming day will be great, and go to sleep with those thoughts in mind.

"End the day with gratitude. There is someone, somewhere that has less than you." - Zig Ziglar

DATE _____

Completed?

SLEEP TARGET FOR TONIGHT: _____ hrs ☐

STRICT LIGHTS OUT TIME FOR TONIGHT: _____ : _____ ☐

OPENING UP ABOUT MY DAY:

_____
_____
_____

MY EVENING ROUTINE FOR TONIGHT:

1. _____ ☐
2. _____ ☐
3. _____ ☐
4. _____ ☐
5. _____ ☐

WHAT'S SOMETHING ON THE BACK OF MY MIND THAT'S STRESSING ME OUT AND WHAT CAN I DO TO ADDRESS IT TOMORROW?

_____
_____

SLEEP EXERCISE TO TRY TONIGHT (OPTIONAL):

IF THOUGHTS ABOUT TASKS OR STRESSORS INTRUDE WHILE YOU TRY TO SLEEP, ACKNOWLEDGE THEM. SAY ALOUD TO YOURSELF, "IT IS TIME FOR REST. I CAN WORK THESE THINGS OUT TOMORROW, BUT FOR NOW, SLEEP IS MY PRIORITY."

Day 49: **Pro-Tip**

Try breath work and meditation.

Breath work and meditation are powerful tools for putting your mind and body in a deeply relaxed state. These methods can decrease your anxiety and stress, while allowing you to get deep rest that gives you an energy boost.

Try this: Put one hand on your chest, and the other hand on your belly. Take a deep breath in and focus on where your breath goes. Does your chest expand, or does your belly expand?

Proper breath work starts at breathing deeply into the belly rather than the chest. This is because breathing into your chest doesn't allow enough air to reach the very bottom parts of your lungs. When you breathe into your belly, your diaphragm acts as a pump to pull oxygen into the bottom of your lungs, allowing for more oxygen intake.

Many meditations combine their voice-guided meditations with breath work, creating a powerful relaxation tactic.

Try this 4-7-8 ratio for your first try at breath work:

- Inhale through your nose for 4 seconds
- Hold your breath for 7 seconds (it's okay if you can't hold it that long yet. It may take time and practice)
- Exhale through your mouth for 8 seconds
- Repeat as many times as you feel necessary

"It's easier to sleep when you don't believe in all the negative thoughts you think." - Jennifer Williamson

DATE _____

Completed?

🛏️ SLEEP TARGET FOR TONIGHT: _____ hrs ☐

💡 STRICT LIGHTS OUT TIME FOR TONIGHT: _____ : _____ ☐

✏️ **OPENING UP ABOUT MY DAY:**

_____
_____
_____

☁️ **MY EVENING ROUTINE FOR TONIGHT:**

1. _____ ☐
2. _____ ☐
3. _____ ☐
4. _____ ☐
5. _____ ☐

💔 **WHERE DO I WANT TO VISIT IN MY DREAMS TONIGHT?**

_____
_____

🛌 **SLEEP EXERCISE TO TRY TONIGHT** (OPTIONAL):

AS YOU CRAWL INTO BED, NOTICE EVERY COMFORTABLE AND PLEASANT SENSATION AND FOCUS ON THEM. FEEL YOUR HEAD SINKING INTO THE PILLOW, THE WARMTH OF YOUR BLANKET, THE SMOOTH SHEETS, ETC.

Day 50: **Pro-Tip**

Exercise early for better sleep.

Early morning workouts, even for just 5 minutes, benefit your body more than you'd think.

For the best benefits, try doing exercises that involve lifting weights. Again, it helps even if your exercises are only for 5 minutes. Lifting weights triggers the production of anabolic hormones, which energize you and promote better sleep later that night.

It doesn't have to happen first thing in the morning, but the earlier you work out, the better sleep you will have that night.

That being said, avoid working out too close to bedtime. If your body secretes these anabolic hormones near bedtime, the energy boost can get in the way of your attempts to fall asleep and stay asleep.

I think the best way to get a good night's sleep is to work hard throughout the day. If you work hard and, of course, work out. Good night."
- William H. McRaven

DATE _____

Completed?

SLEEP TARGET FOR TONIGHT: _____ hrs ☐

STRICT LIGHTS OUT TIME FOR TONIGHT: _____ : _____ ☐

OPENING UP ABOUT MY DAY:

_____

_____

_____

MY EVENING ROUTINE FOR TONIGHT:

(Is there anything in your routine that has become a strong habit and no longer needs to be written?)

1. _____ ☐
2. _____ ☐
3. _____ ☐
4. _____ ☐
5. _____ ☐

WHAT DO I WANT TO TELL MYSELF FIRST THING WHEN I WAKE UP TOMORROW?

_____

_____

SLEEP EXERCISE TO TRY TONIGHT (OPTIONAL):

WHILE IN BED, THINK ABOUT YOUR HAPPIEST MEMORY. CLOSE YOUR EYES AND WATCH THIS MEMORY LIKE A MOVIE. REMEMBER HOW IT MADE YOU FEEL AND NOTICE ALL THE DETAILS. LET THE MEMORY LULL YOU TO SLEEP.

Day 51: **Favorite Resources**

The "Meditation Sidekick Journal" from Habit Nest.

Habit Nest's *Meditation Sidekick Journal* helps you dig deeper into a practice of meditation. Similar to the journal you're holding right now, it guides you through the development of a daily meditation habit using research, tracking, accountability, and resources.

You won't just experience daytime benefits by creating a daily habit of meditating. Incorporating meditation into your daily habits can help your sleep by:

- Easing insomnia and racing thoughts caused by stress, anxiety, and depression
- Improving your ability to cope with stressors
- Quieting thoughts
- Helping you relax your mind and body
- Releasing muscle tension and pain

If you're intrigued by the benefits of meditation and want to look into it further, the *Meditation Sidekick Journal* is the perfect next step!

"Man should forget his anger before he lies down to sleep."
- Mahatma Gandhi

DATE _____

Completed?

🛏️ SLEEP TARGET FOR TONIGHT: _____ hrs ☐

💡 STRICT LIGHTS OUT TIME FOR TONIGHT: _____ : _____ ☐

✏️ **OPENING UP ABOUT MY DAY:**

_____
_____
_____

🌙 **MY EVENING ROUTINE FOR TONIGHT:**

1. _____ ☐
2. _____ ☐
3. _____ ☐
4. _____ ☐
5. _____ ☐

💤 **WHAT OBSTACLES DO I FORESEE GETTING IN THE WAY OF HAVING A GREAT NIGHT'S SLEEP TONIGHT?** (THINK: WHAT DO I NEED TO <u>AVOID</u> DOING?)

_____
_____

🛌 **SLEEP EXERCISE TO TRY TONIGHT** (OPTIONAL):

IF YOU SLEEP BETTER WITH BACKGROUND NOISE, TRY TURNING ON A SOOTHING ASMR VIDEO OR TRACK. DON'T WATCH THE VIDEO, JUST LISTEN AND TRY TO DRIFT OFF.

Day 52: **Pro-Tip**

Morning cold showers, evening hot baths.

When you have the chance, consider trying a combination of cold morning showers and hot evening baths.

In the morning, cold water will help you wake up, become alert, and stimulate your body. It will get you ready to go with a clear, energized mind and body.

When it's time to relax in the evening, try a hot bath. The heat soothes muscle tissue, relaxes your body, and raises your core temperature. That might sound like a bad thing, but you can use it to your advantage.

When you step out of a hot bath, the temperature change causes your core temperature to rapidly decrease. The temperature drop simulates the same natural decrease that prepares your body for bedtime.

A combination of cold showers and hot baths gives you an effective and naturally helpful start and end to your day!

"Rest is the sweet sauce of labor." - Plutarch

DATE _____

Completed?

🛏️ SLEEP TARGET FOR TONIGHT: _____ hrs ☐

💡 STRICT LIGHTS OUT TIME FOR TONIGHT: _____ : _____ ☐

✏️ **OPENING UP ABOUT MY DAY:**

_____
_____
_____

🌙 **MY EVENING ROUTINE FOR TONIGHT:**

1. _____ ☐
2. _____ ☐
3. _____ ☐
4. _____ ☐
5. _____ ☐

💔 **HOW DID I POSITIVELY IMPACT SOMEONE ELSE TODAY?**

_____
_____

🛌 **SLEEP EXERCISE TO TRY TONIGHT** (OPTIONAL):

THINK ABOUT SOMETHING THAT TYPICALLY MAKES YOU FEEL TIRED. IF THE THOUGHT OF COZYING UP BY A FIREPLACE OR WATCHING THE STARS MAKES YOU WANT TO CURL UP IN BED AND SLEEP, THINKING ABOUT IT CAN HELP YOU FEEL SLEEPY.

Day 53: **Pro-Tip**

Prepare to adjust to time changes!

Adjusting to a time change is more than just a minor annoyance. As a matter of fact, hospitals experience a huge increase of heart attacks and other fatigue-related cases when time changes and we lose an hour of sleep.

On the flip side, when the time changes and we gain an hour of sleep, rates of heart attacks and injuries from sleep loss drop drastically.

So what can you do to adjust to these time changes?

- Use melatonin as a temporary circadian rhythm regulator for a day or two while you adjust.
- Adjust your bedtime accordingly to account for the hour of lost or gained sleep.
- Keep yourself awake and alert throughout the day after time changes.
- Be very careful if you experience fatigue and sleepiness that impairs your functioning.

"A sleepy man's eyes generally go to bed some time before he does."
- James Lendall Basford

DATE _____

Completed?

🛌 SLEEP TARGET FOR TONIGHT: _____ hrs ☐

💡 STRICT LIGHTS OUT TIME FOR TONIGHT: _____ : _____ ☐

✏️ **OPENING UP ABOUT MY DAY:**

_____

_____

_____

🌙 **MY EVENING ROUTINE FOR TONIGHT:**

1. _____ ☐
2. _____ ☐
3. _____ ☐
4. _____ ☐
5. _____ ☐

🔄 **WHY IS SLEEPING WELL TONIGHT SO IMPORTANT FOR MY DAY TOMORROW?**

_____

_____

🛏️ **SLEEP EXERCISE TO TRY TONIGHT** (OPTIONAL):

PUT IN A PAIR OF EAR BUDS AND FIND A BINAURAL BEATS TRACK THAT WORKS FOR SLEEP. THESE BEAT PATTERNS ARE THOUGHT TO MANIPULATE YOUR BRAIN INTO FEELING A CERTAIN WAY, INCLUDING FEELING SLEEPY.

Day 54: **Pro-Tip**

Consider replacing your mattress.

No matter how much work you put into your evening routine and sleep schedule, an old, worn out mattress makes for a huge setback in your progress.

Worn out mattresses can disrupt your sleep and create problems with joint pain and stiffness. It makes it hard to have proper sleep posture and prevents you from waking up feeling refreshed.

Ideally, you should replace your mattress every 7-10 years. Some mattresses can be turned to keep it from getting too much wear-and-tear and prolong the use of the mattress.

Finding the right mattress is unique to every single one of us, so do your research, try mattresses in stores as opposed to buying one online, and don't settle for a mattress that you don't absolutely love.

Avoid replacing your mattress with a used one whenever possible!

"A well spent day brings happy sleep." - Leonardo Da Vinci

DATE _____

Completed?

SLEEP TARGET FOR TONIGHT: _____ hrs ☐

STRICT LIGHTS OUT TIME FOR TONIGHT: _____ : _____ ☐

OPENING UP ABOUT MY DAY:

_____
_____
_____

MY EVENING ROUTINE FOR TONIGHT:

1. _____ ☐
2. _____ ☐
3. _____ ☐
4. _____ ☐
5. _____ ☐

WHAT IS SOMETHING I DO DURING THE DAY THAT AFFECTS MY EVENING ROUTINE/SLEEP QUALITY? HOW CAN I CHANGE IT?

_____
_____

SLEEP EXERCISE TO TRY TONIGHT (OPTIONAL):

THINK OF A MOMENT FROM YOUR PAST THAT ALWAYS MADE YOU FEEL BORED AND SLEEPY. FOR EXAMPLE, RESTING YOUR HEAD ON THE DESK IN A COLD CLASSROOM WITH YOUR LEAST FAVORITE SUBJECT BEING TAUGHT.

Day 55: **Favorite Resource**

The "White Noise" app.
Note: we have no affiliation with the White Noise app, we simply think it's a great tool.

For insomniacs or those who get easily distracted or awakened by random sounds, the *White Noise* app is a powerful tool for better sleep.

White Noise has a huge library of sounds that block other disruptive loud noises, while playing a helpful, ambient soundscape to fill the anxiety-inducing silence.

This app is also available for both Android and iOS devices!

"The future seems a little gloomy? Go to bed early, sleep well, eat moderately at breakfast; the future looks brighter. The world's outlook may not have changed, but our capacity for dealing with is has."
- Arthur Lynch

DATE

Completed?

☾ SLEEP TARGET FOR TONIGHT: _____ hrs ☐

💡 STRICT LIGHTS OUT TIME FOR TONIGHT: _____ : _____ ☐

✏️ **OPENING UP ABOUT MY DAY:**

_____
_____
_____

🌙 **MY EVENING ROUTINE FOR TONIGHT:**

1. _____ ☐
2. _____ ☐
3. _____ ☐
4. _____ ☐
5. _____ ☐

💔 **WHAT AM I REALLY HAPPY ABOUT IN MY LIFE?**

_____
_____

🛏️ **SLEEP EXERCISE TO TRY TONIGHT** (OPTIONAL):

TO DECOMPRESS YOUR SPINE AND HELP YOU RELAX, STAND WITH YOUR FEET SPREAD SLIGHTLY PAST YOUR HIPS. LEAN ALL THE WAY FORWARD AND LET YOUR UPPER BODY AND ARMS HANG DOWN. YOU SHOULD FEEL YOUR SPINE LENGTHENING FROM THE PULL OF GRAVITY.

Day 56: **Daily Challenge**

Challenge: Continue to build the habit of shifting between on- and off-days.

As we covered before, it's very common to have failed and missed days as you build an evening routine into your everyday life. One critical value point we hope you're taking away from this experience is building the habit of moving **FROM a point of "failure"** (missing a day or multiple days) **BACK TO the effort of rebuilding this habit.**

That is where the magic happens.

Arguably, missing days make up a critical component of being realistic that you likely won't do an evening routine and get amazing sleep every day for the rest of your life, yet that whenever you want to, you can call on your ability to **SHIFT BACK** into the habit.

That is what this journal is meant to provide you with - the ability to choose and call upon this habit whenever and however often you'd like.

Action step: The next time you fail, remind yourself of the immense long-term value of getting back on track. Remind yourself that building the skill of getting back on track when you've fallen off is one of the primary goals!

"When the going gets tough, the tough take a nap." - Tom Hodgkinson

DATE _____

Completed?

SLEEP TARGET FOR TONIGHT: _____ hrs ☐

STRICT LIGHTS OUT TIME FOR TONIGHT: _____ : _____ ☐

OPENING UP ABOUT MY DAY:

_____

_____

_____

MY EVENING ROUTINE FOR TONIGHT:

1. _____ ☐
2. _____ ☐
3. _____ ☐
4. _____ ☐
5. _____ ☐

WHAT DO I NEED TO CHANGE IN REGARDS TO MY HABITS WITH SOCIAL APPS / GAMING / ENTERTAINMENT TO IMPROVE MY SLEEP?

_____

_____

SLEEP EXERCISE TO TRY TONIGHT (OPTIONAL):

TRY BRUSHING YOUR TEETH AND WASHING YOUR FACE 30-60 MINUTES BEFORE BED. THE BRIGHT BATHROOM LIGHTS AND COMMON MINT-FLAVORED TOOTHPASTE CAN ACTUALLY MAKE YOU FEEL MORE AWAKE.

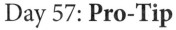

Day 57: **Pro-Tip**

<u>*Save a life, don't drive drowsy.*</u>

Choosing not to get behind the wheel of a vehicle while drowsy could very well save a life. Even if you don't realize how drowsy you are, you can still experience episodes of micro-sleeps. All it takes is a split second of micro-sleep for something devastating to occur.

These statistics and facts surrounding drowsy driving are shocking and shed new light on an often ignored, dangerous choice:

- 19 hours of sleep deprivation is enough to make you as cognitively impaired as someone considered legally drunk.
- Being drowsy makes you 3 times more likely to get in a wreck.
- In North America, drowsy driving accounts for an estimated 328,000 accidents annually, with over 6,000 fatalities.
- Not including damage to property, the annual economic toll of drowsy driving accidents, injuries, and fatalities is around $109 BILLION.

Injuring someone else from drowsy driving definitely isn't something you want weighing on your conscience. You are loved and appreciated as well, so those who love you need you safe and alive! Save a life and don't get behind the wheel if you're drowsy.

"It is better to sleep on things beforehand than lie awake about them afterwards." - Baltasar Gracian

DATE _____

Completed?

🛏️ SLEEP TARGET FOR TONIGHT: _____ hrs ☐

💡 STRICT LIGHTS OUT TIME FOR TONIGHT: _____ : _____ ☐

✏️ **OPENING UP ABOUT MY DAY:**

_____
_____
_____

🌙 **MY EVENING ROUTINE FOR TONIGHT:**

1. _____ ☐
2. _____ ☐
3. _____ ☐
4. _____ ☐
5. _____ ☐

💔 **HOW DOES MY QUALITY OF SLEEP AFFECT MY MOOD? DOES THIS HAVE ANY SNOWBALL EFFECTS ON MY DAY I SHOULD BE MINDFUL OF?**

_____
_____

🛌 **SLEEP EXERCISE TO TRY TONIGHT** (OPTIONAL):

TRY RECITING THE ALPHABET BACKWARDS TO FALL ASLEEP. IF YOU MAKE A MISTAKE OR LOSE YOUR PLACE, START OVER. BREATHE IN AND OUT SLOWLY AS YOU GO.

Day 58: **Daily Challenge**

Challenge: Try practicing Yoga Nidra.

It might sound like a workout, but Yoga Nidra is actually a form of guided meditation. It's meant to help you sleep by putting you in a "yogic sleep," which is a state of consciousness between being awake and the early stages of sleep.

Several studies have shown that Yoga Nidra improves sleep quality and alleviates chronic insomnia. It helps your body fully relax and release anxiety and stress.

Some Yoga Nidra CDs and audio tracks are available to purchase, but there are also a ton of free tracks online, on *YouTube*, and in several apps.

Tonight, find a Yoga Nidra track. When you lie down in bed, start the track (preferably with headphones or ear buds). Close your eyes and follow the track. Allow it to lull you to sleep.

When you wake up, think about how you feel. Did you sleep any better? Do you feel more refreshed? If so, consider adding Yoga Nidra to your bedtime routine.

"The way to a more productive, more inspired, more joyful life is getting enough sleep." - Arianna Huffington

DATE _____

Completed?

🛏 SLEEP TARGET FOR TONIGHT: _____ hrs ☐

💡 STRICT LIGHTS OUT TIME FOR TONIGHT: _____ : _____ ☐

✏ **OPENING UP ABOUT MY DAY:**

_____

_____

_____

🌙 **MY EVENING ROUTINE FOR TONIGHT:**

1. _____ ☐
2. _____ ☐
3. _____ ☐
4. _____ ☐
5. _____ ☐

↻ **WHAT EXTRA PREP-WORK CAN I DO TONIGHT THAT WOULD IMPROVE MY DAY TOMORROW?**

_____

_____

🛌 **SLEEP EXERCISE TO TRY TONIGHT** (OPTIONAL):

IF WORRIES ARISE WHILE YOU'RE TRYING TO SLEEP, IMAGINE PLACING THEM, ON-BY-ONE, IN A CHEST. IF THE WORRIES ARE NEEDLESS, THROW THEM AWAY. WHEN YOU'RE DONE, MENTALLY LOCK THIS CHEST AND REVISIT IT TOMORROW.

Day 59: **Pro-Tip**

Use a HEPA air filter & a quiet humidifier in your bedroom.

If the air in your bedroom is accumulating allergens or is too dry, this could have your sleep quality really suffering. These conditions can cause some super uncomfortable symptoms like eye itching and watering, sinus congestion, coughing, and/or dry mouth and sinuses.

1. Keep pollen, dust, dander, and other allergens out of the air with any air purifier with a HEPA filter.

If dry winter air (or dry air in high altitude areas) is drying out your sinuses, you might have trouble comfortably falling asleep.

2. Use a quiet humidifier in your bedroom to moisten the air.

Other ways to keep the air clean include washing your bedding, vacuum, or sweep and mop in your room once weekly.

"When I'm worried and cannot sleep, I count my blessings instead of sheep." - Bing Crosby

DATE _____

Completed?

🛏 SLEEP TARGET FOR TONIGHT: _____ hrs ☐

💡 STRICT LIGHTS OUT TIME FOR TONIGHT: _____ : _____ ☐

✏️ **OPENING UP ABOUT MY DAY:**

_____

_____

_____

🌥 **MY EVENING ROUTINE FOR TONIGHT:**

1. _____ ☐
2. _____ ☐
3. _____ ☐
4. _____ ☐
5. _____ ☐

💤 **WHAT'S SOMETHING ON THE BACK OF MY MIND THAT'S STRESSING ME OUT AND WHAT CAN I DO TO ADDRESS IT TOMORROW?**

_____

_____

🛌 **SLEEP EXERCISE TO TRY TONIGHT** (OPTIONAL):

IF YOU LIKE BACKGROUND NOISE, HAVE SOOTHING MUSIC (LIKE CLASSICAL MUSIC) PLAYING SOFTLY WHILE YOU FALL ASLEEP.

Day 60: **Food For Thought**

The benefits of cognitive behavioral therapy.

If you struggle with insomnia symptoms like difficulty falling asleep and staying asleep, cognitive behavioral therapy (CBT) can help alleviate some of those symptoms.

Therapy often gathers negative stigma and connotations, but think of CBT as a doctor's visit for the mind. Just the same as you need to see a doctor to stay in good physical health and address any issues, your mental health needs similar visits and check-ups as well.

CBT often includes consistent, regular visits to a psychologist or psychiatrist. They'll be able to assess your evening routine, assign a sleep diary, and help you confront any mental/emotional factors that might be getting in the way.

CBT is proven through research to help you fall asleep, stay asleep, and improve your sleep quality. If you feel that CBT could help you, go for it! Taking care of your mental health is enormously important, so don't feel ashamed - feel brave proud of yourself for recognizing what you need and acting on it!

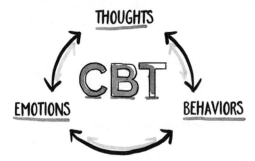

"A day without a nap is like a cupcake without frosting."
- Terri Guillemets

DATE _____

Completed?

🛏️ SLEEP TARGET FOR TONIGHT: _____ hrs ☐

💡 STRICT LIGHTS OUT TIME FOR TONIGHT: ____ : ____ ☐

✏️ **OPENING UP ABOUT MY DAY:**

_____
_____
_____

☁️ **MY EVENING ROUTINE FOR TONIGHT:**

1. _____ ☐
2. _____ ☐
3. _____ ☐
4. _____ ☐
5. _____ ☐

💔 **WHERE DO I WANT TO VISIT IN MY DREAMS TONIGHT?**

_____
_____

🛌 **SLEEP EXERCISE TO TRY TONIGHT** (OPTIONAL):

FIND A PODCAST THAT WON'T KEEP YOU DISTRACTED AND ALLOW IT TO PLAY AS YOU CLOSE YOUR EYES AND TRY TO SLEEP.

Day 61: **Affirmations**

<u>Celebrating the journey.</u>

1. Find a quiet area where you can do this in private so you can be at ease. If you can't find a private space, say this in your head.
2. Think of a time when you felt absolutely relaxed, calm, and pleasant.
3. As you say the following words, imagine yourself in a place that makes you feel incredibly at ease.

I have made it so far in my journey, and each night gets me closer to my goals. I am developing a healthy, life-long relationship with sleep and seeing a bounty of positive effects from it. I am happy with where I am in life, and proud of how far I have come. I trust myself to make positive decisions about my sleep moving forward. I am now ready to rest deeply, free of responsibilities and associations.

Repeat this **one more time.**

"There is more refreshment and stimulation in a nap, even of the briefest, than in all the alcohol ever distilled." - Edward Lucas

DATE _____

Completed?

🛏️ SLEEP TARGET FOR TONIGHT: _____ hrs ☐

💡 STRICT LIGHTS OUT TIME FOR TONIGHT: _____ : _____ ☐

✏️ **OPENING UP ABOUT MY DAY:**

_____

_____

_____

🌙 **MY EVENING ROUTINE FOR TONIGHT:**

1. _____ ☐
2. _____ ☐
3. _____ ☐
4. _____ ☐
5. _____ ☐

🔄 **WHAT DO I WANT TO TELL MYSELF FIRST THING WHEN I WAKE UP TOMORROW?**

_____

_____

🛌 **SLEEP EXERCISE TO TRY TONIGHT** (OPTIONAL):

TAKE A WARM BATH WITH EPSOM SALT. IF POSSIBLE, TRY EPSOM SALT WITH ESSENTIAL OILS ALREADY IN THEM. THE EPSOM SALT WILL HELP YOUR MUSCLES FURTHER RELAX.

Day 62: **Pro-Tip**

Spend as little time awake in bed as possible.

While training your body to respond to your evening sleep cues, it's important to make sure that your brain only associates your room and bed with sleep. The way your brain associates certain places with specific mental and physical feelings can either be a giant hurdle, or a powerful tool.

If you frequently spend a few minutes lying awake in your bed before getting up, or you spend more than 20 minutes lying in bed awake at night, your brain begins to associate your bed with being awake and alert - or with the stress and anxiety of not being able to fall asleep.

To combat this and change the way your brain perceives your room and bed, try:

Getting out of bed as soon as you wake up.

Getting out of bed at night if you have been lying down for 15-20 minutes without falling asleep. You don't have to spend a ton of time out of bed - as that would end up working against you - but you can use this time to find a screen-free relaxing activity to help you get closer to sleep.

"If you can't sleep, then get up and do something instead of lying there worrying. It's the worry that gets you, not the lack of sleep."
- Dale Carnegie

_____

DATE

Completed?

🛏️ SLEEP TARGET FOR TONIGHT: _____ hrs ☐

💡 STRICT LIGHTS OUT TIME FOR TONIGHT: _____ : _____ ☐

✏️ **OPENING UP ABOUT MY DAY:**

_____

_____

_____

🌥️ **MY EVENING ROUTINE FOR TONIGHT:**

1. _____ ☐
2. _____ ☐
3. _____ ☐
4. _____ ☐
5. _____ ☐

💤 **WHAT OBSTACLES DO I FORESEE GETTING IN THE WAY OF HAVING A GREAT NIGHT'S SLEEP TONIGHT?** (THINK: WHAT DO I NEED TO <u>AVOID</u> DOING?)

_____

_____

🛌 **SLEEP EXERCISE TO TRY TONIGHT** (OPTIONAL):

NEED TO REMEMBER SOMETHING IMPORTANT? REPEAT IT MULTIPLE TIMES RIGHT BEFORE FALLING ASLEEP. COME UP WITH MNEMONICS. WHILE ASLEEP, YOUR BRAIN WILL CONSOLIDATE THE INFORMATION INTO YOUR MEMORY.

Day 63: **Daily Challenge**

Challenge: Avoid nicotine before bed.

If you consume any tobacco or nicotine products before bed, this could be delaying the onset of sleep or disrupting sleep continuity.

In fact, research from Florida Atlantic University found that nicotine worsens sleep onset and continuity by 43 minutes, on average. Getting 43 minutes less of sleep doesn't sound like a big deal, but it makes a bigger difference than you might think!

So, how exactly does nicotine interfere with sleep?

- Nicotine has stimulant properties.
- The airway irritation caused by smoke inhalation can raise your risk of developing sleep apnea.
- You can experience nicotine withdrawal symptoms while you sleep, which can have you waking up multiple times feeling agitated.

Challenge yourself to avoid products containing nicotine before bed. Ideally, nicotine should be nixed 2 hours before bedtime. You can work your way toward 2 hours over time if you struggle too much with going to 2 hours right off-the-bat.

"Insomnia is an indication, not a chaos. It's like ache. You're not going to provide a patient ache medicine without figuring out what's reasoning the pain." - Judith Owens

_____
DATE

Completed?

🛏️ SLEEP TARGET FOR TONIGHT: _____ hrs ☐

💡 STRICT LIGHTS OUT TIME FOR TONIGHT: _____ : _____ ☐

✏️ **OPENING UP ABOUT MY DAY:**

_____
_____
_____

🌥️ **MY EVENING ROUTINE FOR TONIGHT:**

1. _____ ☐
2. _____ ☐
3. _____ ☐
4. _____ ☐
5. _____ ☐

💔 **HOW DID I POSITIVELY IMPACT SOMEONE ELSE TODAY?**

_____
_____

🛌 **SLEEP EXERCISE TO TRY TONIGHT** (OPTIONAL):

TENSE NECK AND SHOULDERS? DRAPE A RAG SOAKED IN HOT WATER AROUND YOUR NECK AND SHOULDERS. PRACTICE SOME DEEP BREATHING AND FOCUS ON LETTING THOSE MUSCLES RELAX.

Day 64: **Pro-Tip**

<u>Weighted Blankets.</u>

If you struggle with insomnia that's secondary to stress, anxiety, or depression, research suggest that using a weighted blanket could be a solid solution.

The pressure and warmth from a weighted blanket helps you feel soothed and secure, making it easier for your body and mind to relax. It also reduces the barrage of sensory stimulation that can come from the movement of regular blankets, making it especially suitable for those that are prone to sensory overload.

Weighted blankets come in a range of weight, anywhere from 5-30 pounds. When choosing a blanket, it's important to pick a weight that best suits your own body size and weight.

For adults weighing between 165-200 pounds, a 20 pound weighted blanket should do the trick. Adults weighing above 200 should ideally find a blanket in the 25-30 pound range. If you're still not sure, a solid rule of thumb is to pick a blanket that weighs around 10% of your body weight.

As a bonus, it's also great to wear a weighted eye mask if you're prone to headaches or built-up sinus pressure. A 0.5 pound weighted eye mask is sure to do the trick without feeling uncomfortably heavy.

"A little insomnia is not without its value in making us appreciate sleep, in throwing a ray of light upon that darkness." - Marcel Proust

DATE _____

Completed?

🛏️ SLEEP TARGET FOR TONIGHT: _____ hrs ☐

💡 STRICT LIGHTS OUT TIME FOR TONIGHT: _____ : _____ ☐

✏️ **OPENING UP ABOUT MY DAY:**

_____
_____
_____

🌙 **MY EVENING ROUTINE FOR TONIGHT:**

1. _____ ☐
2. _____ ☐
3. _____ ☐
4. _____ ☐
5. _____ ☐

↻ **WHY IS SLEEPING WELL TONIGHT SO IMPORTANT FOR MY DAY TOMORROW?**

_____
_____

🛌 **SLEEP EXERCISE TO TRY TONIGHT** (OPTIONAL):

REMOVE ANY VISIBLE CLOCK FACES IN YOUR ROOM TO ELIMINATE "CLOCK WATCHING." IF YOU NEED YOUR DIGITAL ALARM, TURN IT AROUND SO YOU CAN'T SEE THE TIME.

Day 65: Daily Challenge

Challenge: Try acupressure.

Although research on the health benefits of acupressure is still in early stages, current research has shown promising results.

Acupressure is believed to promote well-being and relieve symptoms of migraines, fatigue, anxiety, depression, insomnia, back pain, stress, and insomnia.

In the case of insomnia, there are 3 specific acupressure points you can do while lying in bed - the spirit gate, the inner frontier gate, and the wind pool. For each spot, apply gentle pressure to the points and massage with a circular or up-and-down movement for 2-3 minutes..

- To find the spirit gate, try feeling for a little hollow space on your wrist directly below your palm on the pinky finger side of your hand. Repeat this on your other wrist.
- For the inner frontier gate, turn one palm face up. Measure 3 finger-widths below the crease of your wrist. Apply pressure in the center between the 2 tendons and repeat on your other arm.
- To locate the wind pool spot, create a cup or bowl shape with your hands by interlocking your fingers and opening both palms. Position the cup made by your hands at the base of you skull with your thumbs applying pressure to both sides of the base.

Keep in mind that acupressure should be avoided by pregnant women and anyone with high blood pressure.

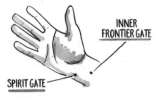

"Sometimes the most urgent and vital thing you can possibly do is take a complete rest." - Ashleigh Brilliant

DATE _____

Completed?

🛏️ SLEEP TARGET FOR TONIGHT: _____ hrs ☐

💡 STRICT LIGHTS OUT TIME FOR TONIGHT: _____ : _____ ☐

✏️ **OPENING UP ABOUT MY DAY:**

_____
_____
_____

🌙 **MY EVENING ROUTINE FOR TONIGHT:**

1. _____ ☐
2. _____ ☐
3. _____ ☐
4. _____ ☐
5. _____ ☐

💤 **WHAT IS SOMETHING I DO DURING THE DAY THAT AFFECTS MY EVENING ROUTINE/SLEEP QUALITY? HOW CAN I CHANGE IT?**

_____
_____

🛌 **SLEEP EXERCISE TO TRY TONIGHT** (OPTIONAL):

FOR 30-60 MINUTES BEFORE BED, FIND A RELAXING SCREEN-FREE ACTIVITY TO DO. TURN OFF ANY ARTIFICIAL LIGHTING AND DO THIS ACTIVITY BY CANDLELIGHT.

Phase 3 Medal Earned!

Day 66: **Congratulations!!!** 🥂

You've made it to the end of the journal!!

For you to have gotten this far means you've earned a very serious congratulations. You need to celebrate because your willpower and confidence should be soaring through the roof. You've gained lessons about yourself not many dare to approach. You've struggled with your own mind, body and heart and gained some serious control over them. You fully understand that you have the power in you to accomplish ANY goal you put your mind to.

This is a skill you've built inside you that you can turn on whenever you need it at any future point in your lifetime. **That's so awesome.**

You are a WARRIOR and we (Amir, Ari, & Mikey) hope you continue to build on your habit success and personal development for the rest of your life.

Note: We LOVE sharing stories of our users and what their lives looked like BEFORE using the journal compared to where they are NOW!

If you want to share your story with us, you can do so here:
habitnest.com/sleeptestimonial

DATE _____

Completed?

🛌 SLEEP TARGET FOR TONIGHT: _____ hrs ☐

💡 STRICT LIGHTS OUT TIME FOR TONIGHT: _____ : _____ ☐

✏️ **OPENING UP ABOUT MY DAY:**

_____
_____
_____

🌙 **MY EVENING ROUTINE FOR TONIGHT:**

1. _____ ☐
2. _____ ☐
3. _____ ☐
4. _____ ☐
5. _____ ☐

💔 **WHAT AM I REALLY HAPPY ABOUT IN MY LIFE?**

_____
_____

🛏️ **SLEEP EXERCISE TO TRY TONIGHT** (OPTIONAL):

SPEND A FEW MINUTES BEFORE BED MASSAGING YOUR BODY AND MUSCLES WITH A MOISTURIZING LOTION, PREFERABLY WITH A PLEASANT, CALMING SCENT.

~~PHASE 3.~~ MASTERED.

Phase 3 Recap: Days 22-66+

1. Think about what your life looked like before you began this habit - what are you doing differently now? How do you feel?

\
\
\
\

2. What unforeseen effects has your life gained from all this?

\
\
\
\

3. When you are struggling with this habit in the future, what are the key factors you should remember to do again?

\
\
\
\

4. What daily tracking & accountability can you have going forward to maintain the momentum you've built here?

\
\

- *Fin* -

So... What Now?

Although you should feel very accomplished for getting through this entire journal... know that you built this habit to *continually improve your life. Don't stop now. This is only the beginning.*

One huge factor to this is tracking your progress. Once you stop tracking, it makes it exponentially easier for you to skip staying consistent (due to the lack of accountability with yourself).

Remember: **Every single day in your life that you greet well-rested and performing at your best will automatically be a better day of your life.**

You only stand to gain from continuing this habit.

Meet the Habit Nest Cofounders

Amir Atighehchi graduated from USC's Marshall School of Business in 2013. He got his first taste of entrepreneurship during college with Mikey when they co-founded a bicycle lock company called *Nutlock*. It wasn't until after college when he opened his eyes to the world of personal development and healthy habits. Amir is fascinated by creative challenges and entrepreneurship.

Mikey Ahdoot transformed his life from a 200+ pound video game addict to someone who was completing 17 daily habits consistently at one point. From ice cold showers to brainstorming 10 ideas a day (shoutout to James Altucher) to celebrating life every single day, he is first-hand becoming a habit routine machine that sets himself up for success daily. He is a graduate of USC's Marshall School of Business and a proud Trojan.

Ari Banayan graduated from the University of Southern California Gould School of Law in 2016. Through his own life experience, he understands how important it is to take care of ourselves mentally, physically and emotionally to operate at maximum capacity. He uses waking up early, reading, meditation, exercise, and a healthy diet to create a solid foundation for his everyday life.

Read all of our full stories here:
habitnest.com/about-us

Shop Habit Nest Products

Lifestyle Products

All of our lifestyle journals come with **daily content** (including Pro-Tips, Daily Challenges, Practical Resources, & more) to inspire you and give you bite-sized information to use along your journey. They also contain **daily questions aimed at holding you accountable** to ingraining that habit into your life.

- **The Morning Sidekick Journal Series**
  A set of guided morning planners that help you conquer your mornings and conquer your life. This complete 4-volume series covers 1-year of morning routines.

- **The Evening Routine & Sleep Sidekick Journal**
  Helps you to wind down your days peacefully, prepare for each next day, and get the most rejuvenating sleep of your life.

- **The Gratitude Sidekick Journal**
  A research-based journal that will help make an **attitude of appreciation** a core part of who you are.

- **The Meditation Sidekick Journal**
  Built to give you all the tools you need to stay consistent with a meditation practice.

- **The Nutrition Sidekick Journal**
  Your nutrition tracker, informational guide, and coach, all in one.

- **The Budgeting Sidekick Journal Series**
  The most simple-yet-effective budgeting guide in the world, helping you find full clarity on your budgeting goals and to achieve financial freedom. Set spending goals, track your daily spending, and reconcile along the way. Contains 2 volumes which cover well over a year of budgeting.

Fitness Products

Our no-nonsense fitness books have fully guided fitness routines.
No thinking required; just open the books and follow along.

- **The Weightlifting Gym Buddy Journal Series**
A set of guided personal training programs aimed at helping you have the best workouts of your life. This complete 4-volume series covers 1-year of weightlifting workouts.

- **The Bodyweight / Dumbbell Home Workout Journals**
Specifically focus on HOME workout programs that require minimal-to-no equipment to complete.

- **The Badass Body Goals Journal**
An at-home-friendly fitness journal that focuses on HIIT and circuit workouts. This journal comes with a full video guide you can play and follow along.

Other Products

- **The Habit Nest Mobile Application**
The app will offer a digital representation of our journals so you can stay on your Habit Nest journey while mobile. Available on iOS & Android.

- **The Habit Nest Daily Planner**
Plan your day including your top priorities, smaller 5-minute tasks, and all your to-dos. Get optional suggestions for ways to start your mornings and end your evenings with as well.

- **George The Short-Necked Giraffe (Children's Book)**
Follow along George's journey as he learns the hard way that fully accepting himself, exactly the way he is, is the only path to living his happiest life.

Shop all products here: **habitnest.com/store**

Share The Love

If you're reading this, that means you've come pretty far from where you were when starting. You should be extremely proud of yourself!

If you believe this journal has had a positive impact on your life, we invite you to consider gifting a new one to a friend.

Is there a holiday coming up? Is there a special birthday around the corner? Or do you just want to put a smile on someone's face and do something incredible for them?

Gifting this journal is the absolute best way to show any gratitude you may have for what we've written here, as well as serving as a force of good through giving back to others. And you can rest assured that you're helping improve another person's life at the same time.

We created a discount code for getting this far that can be used for any Habit Nest product (make sure to use the same email address you placed the order with).

If you decide to, feel free to re-order here:
https://habitnest.com

Use code **Sleepy15** for 15% off!

The Habit Nest Mobile App

When Habit Nest was initially founded, it was supposed to be in mobile app form from the start. We tried for a year as a team of three young founders with no outside funding to get a mobile app built, but we never could pull it off back then.

We switched to paper journals that worked using the same concept, which you're currently holding. Now, 5 years and hundreds of thousands of journals sold later, **we're finally in a place to chase our dream** of creating an app.

It's making us a bit emotional as things have come full circle and we're unbelievably **thankful for every single customer (like you)** who has helped us get here, shared their ups and downs with us, and really just **given us a chance** to grow our little company that sincerely cares.

We've been working extremely hard to be able to create the Habit Nest mobile app this year and **it will be live in the iOS and Android app stores in January 2021.**

The app will offer a **digital representation of our journals** so you can stay on your Habit Nest journey while mobile.

If you're interested in seeing how it can help you, feel free to see more at **habitnest.com/app**

Thank you for making this possible.

With hugs and a lot of love,
Mikey Ahdoot, Ari Banayan, & Amir Atighehchi
Cofounders of Habit Nest

Content Index

Day 1: Pro-Tip - Make a non-negotiable list.

Day 2: Daily Challenge - Cleanse your room of electronics.

Day 3: Food For Thought - Think of sleep as a valuable resource and necessity.

Day 4: Daily Challenge - Create an optimal sleep sanctuary.

Day 5: Pro-Tip - Consistency is the key.

Day 6: Daily Challenge - Try doing your 3 MITs first thing in the morning.

Day 7: Affirmations - Worthy of rest.

Day 8: Daily Challenge - Avoid sugar in the evening.

Day 9: Favorite Resources - Try nasal strips to open your nasal passages and to help breathe through your nose as you sleep.

Day 10: Pro-Tip - Blue light blockers.

Day 11: Favorite Resources - Recommended app: Shortcuts for iPhone.

Day 12: Pro-Tip - Combatting racing thoughts.

Day 13: Daily Challenge - Scale back on caffeine.

Day 14: Food For Thought - Your evening willpower.

Day 15: Daily Challenge - The "chairman of the board" exercise.

Day 16: Pro-Tip - Communicate about your sleep schedule.

Day 17: Pro-Tip - A natural bedtime sleep remedy.

Day 18: Favorite Resources - Try activating your vagus nerve.

Day 19: Pro-Tip - Take advantage of your sleep window.

Day 20: Pro-Tip - The power of "power naps."

Day 21: Food For Thought - Supplements for sleep.

Day 22: Pro-Tip - Black out your room.

Day 23: Food For Thought - Reflect on the impact.

Day 24: Affirmations - Calming your mind.

Day 25: Pro-Tip - Keep your mattress cool.

Day 26: Food For Thought - The pros and cons of cellphones.

Day 27: Pro-Tip - Light can throw off your sleep.

Day 28: Pro-Tip - Try a buckwheat pillow.

Day 29: Affirmations - Inhale, exhale.

Day 30: Pro-Tip - Handling social "jet lag."

Day 31: Pro-Tip - Wearable sleep trackers.

Day 32: Pro-Tip - Avoid alcohol and certain medications before bed.

Day 33: Favorite Resources - Recommended app: SleepScore.

Day 34: Daily Challenge - Practice good sleep posture.

Day 35: Pro-Tip - Get your vitamin and mineral levels checked.

Day 36: Pro-Tip - Do a "closing ritual" to separate your work day from your evening.

Day 37: Daily Challenge - Try the Wim Hof method.

Day 38: Pro-Tip - Helpful phone features.

Day 39: Pro-Tip - Sleep and your diet.

Day 40: Daily Challenge - Implement a phone curfew.

Day 41: Pro-Tip - Try a light therapy lamp.

Day 42: Pro-Tip - Consider ditching your alarm.

Day 43: Food For Thought - Start a "worry" journal.

Day 44: Pro-Tip - Let music soothe you to sleep.

Day 45: Super Read - "Why We Sleep" by Matthew Walker.

Day 46: Pro-Tip - Don't over-schedule yourself.

Day 47: Pro-Tip - Bring your pets to bed.

Day 48: Daily Challenge - Practice gratitude before bed.

Day 49: Pro-Tip - Try breath work and meditation.

Day 50: Pro-Tip - Exercise early for better sleep.

Day 51: Favorite Resources - The "Meditation Sidekick Journal" from Habit Nest.

Day 52: Pro-Tip - Morning cold showers, evening hot showers.

Day 53: Pro-Tip - Prepare to adjust to time change!

Day 54: Pro-Tip - Replacing your mattress.

Day 55: Favorite Resource - The "White Noise" app.

Day 56: Daily Challenge - Continue to build the habit of shifting between on- and off-days.

Day 57: Pro-Tip - Save a life, don't drive drowsy.

Day 58: Daily Challenge - Try practicing Yoga Nidra.

Day 59: Double Pro-Tip - Use a HEPA air filter & a quiet humidifier in your bedroom.

Day 60: Food For Thought - The benefits of cognitive behavioral therapy.

Day 61: Affirmations - Celebrating the journey.

Day 62: Pro-Tip - Spend as little time awake in bed as possible.

Day 63: Daily Challenge - Avoid nicotine before bed.

Day 64: Pro-Tip - Weighted blankets.

Day 65: Daily Challenge - Try acupressure.

Day 66: Congratulations!!!

How Was This Journal Created?

We formulated the journal as a mix between what we find personally effective through our own experience as well as through researching published scientific material and books on the newest, most relevant information we could find.

The following is a mix of studies we used to formulate the journal - some points take ideas found in some sources and mix them with our own experience or with other research points.

Some of the main sources of inspiration came from:

It is a bit difficult to assign specific studies to specific pages in the book as there is a decent amount of overlap in different sections, though we will do our best.

The "Why"

Fishbach, Ayelet, and Ravi Dhar. "Goals as Excuses or Guides: The Liberating Effect of Perceived Goal Progress on Choice." Journal of Consumer Research, vol. 32, no. 3, 2005, pp. 370–377., doi:10.1086/497548.

The "What"

Gardner, Benjamin, et al. "Making Health Habitual: the Psychology of 'Habit-Formation' and General Practice." British Journal of General Practice, vol. 62, no. 605, 2012, pp. 664–666., doi:10.3399/bjgp12x659466.

The "Why"

Huffington, Arianna Stassinopoulos. The Sleep Revolution. Harmony Books, 2016, p. 28.

IBM. "IBM 2010 Global CEO Study: Creativity Selected As Most Crucial Factor For Future Success". IBM News Room, 2010, https://newsroom.ibm.com/2010-05-18-IBM-2010-Global-CEO-Study-Creativity-Selected-as-Most-Crucial-Factor-for-Future-Success?mhsrc=ibmsearch_a&mhq=2010%20CEO%20Survey.

Söderström, M., Jeding, K., Ekstedt, M., Perski, A., & Åkerstedt, T. (2012). Insufficient sleep predicts clinical burnout. Journal of Occupational Health Psychology, 17(2), 175–183. https://doi.org/10.1037/a0027518

UCLA. "Coping With Shift Work - UCLA Sleep Disorders Center - Los Angeles, CA". Uclahealth.Org, https://www.uclahealth.org/sleepcenter/coping-with-shift-work.

Walker, Matthew. Why We Sleep. Penguin Books, 2017

What To Expect

Breus, Michael. 10 Things Great Sleepers Do. 2015, p. 1, https://thesleepdoctor.com/wp-content/uploads/2015/12/10-things-great-sleepers-do.pdf.

Canadian Centre for Occupational Health and Safety. "Rotational Shiftwork : OSH Answers". Ccohs.Ca, 2020, https://www.ccohs.ca/oshanswers/ergonomics/shiftwrk.html.

The "How"

American Sleep Apnea Association. "Sleep Apnea Information For Clinicians – Sleep Apnea". Sleepapnea.Org, https://www.sleepapnea.org/learn/sleep-apnea-information-clinicians/.

Breus, Michael. 10 Things Great Sleepers Do. 2015, p. 4-5, https://thesleepdoctor.com/wp-content/uploads/2015/12/10-things-great-sleepers-do.pdf.

Brooks, R. (2017). How to Diagnose & Treat the 5 Most Common Sleep Disorders. Aastweb.org. Retrieved from https://www.aastweb.org/blog/how-to-diagnose-treat-the-5-most-common-sleep-disorders.

Tangney, June P., et al. "High Self-Control Predicts Good Adjustment, Less Pathology, Better Grades, and Interpersonal Success." Journal of Personality, vol. 72, no. 2, 2004, pp. 271–324., doi:10.1111/j.0022-3506.2004.00263.x.

Tracking Pages

Fishbach, Ayelet, and Ravi Dhar. "Goals as Excuses or Guides: The Liberating Effect of Perceived Goal Progress on Choice." Journal of Consumer Research, vol. 32, no. 3, 2005, pp. 370–377., doi:10.1086/497548.

Fogg, BJ. "What Causes Behavior Change?" *BJ Fogg's Behavior Model*, www.behaviormodel.org/index.html.

Daily Content

Alexander, E. (2020). Apple Cider Vinegar and Honey for Sleep: A Fact or A Myth? - Sleep Report. Sleep Report. Retrieved from https://sleep.report/apple-cider-vinegar-and-honey-for-sleep/.

Bent, S., Padula, A., Moore, D., Patterson, M., & Mehling, W. (2006). Valerian for Sleep: A Systematic Review and Meta-Analysis. The American Journal Of Medicine, 119(12), 1005-1012. https://doi.org/10.1016/j.amjmed.2006.02.026

Bray, R. (1999). Massage: Exploring the benefits. Harrow On The Hill, 11(5), 15.

Breus, Michael. 10 Things Great Sleepers Do. 2015, https://thesleepdoctor.com/wp-content/uploads/2015/12/10-things-great-sleepers-do.pdf.

Breus, Michael., & Oz, M. (2016). The Power of When. Little, Brown, and Company.

Calvin, A., Carter, R., Adachi, T., Macedo, P., Albuquerque, F., & van der Walt, C. et al. (2013). Effects of Experimental Sleep Restriction on Caloric Intake and Activity Energy Expenditure. Chest, 144(1), 79-86. https://doi.org/10.1378/chest.12-2829

Chang, E., Lai, H., Chen, P., Hsieh, Y., & Lee, L. (2012). The effects of music on the sleep quality of adults with chronic insomnia using evidence from polysomnographic and self-reported analysis: A randomized control trial. International Journal Of Nursing Studies, 49(8), 921-930. https://doi.org/10.1016/j.ijnurstu.2012.02.019

Covington, T. (2020). Drowsy Driving Statistics. Thezebra.com. Retrieved from https://www.thezebra.com/research/drowsy-driving-statistics/.

Datta, K., Tripathi, M. & Mallick, H.N. Yoga Nidra: An innovative approach for management of chronic insomnia- A case report. Sleep Science Practice 1, 7 (2017). https://doi.org/10.1186/s41606-017-0009-4

Djokic, G., Vojvodic, P., Korcok, D., Agic, A., Rankovic, A., & Djordjevic, V. et al. (2019). The Effects of Magnesium – Melatonin - Vit B Complex Supplementation in Treatment of Insomnia. Open Access Macedonian Journal Of Medical Sciences, 7(18), 3101-3105. https://doi.org/10.3889/oamjms.2019.771

Ekholm, B., Spulber, S., & Adler, M. (2020). A randomized controlled study of weighted chain blankets for insomnia in psychiatric disorders. Journal Of Clinical Sleep Medicine. https://doi.org/10.5664/jcsm.8636

Fallis, Jordan. (2017). How to Stimulate Your Vagus Nerve for Better Mental Health [Ebook]. Retrieved 27 August 2020, from https://sass.uottawa.ca/sites/sass.uottawa.ca/files/how_to_stimulate_your_vagus_nerve_for_better_mental_health_1.pdf.

Fritz, S., & Gold, B. (2003). Buckwheat pillow-induced asthma and allergic rhinitis. Annals Of Allergy, Asthma & Immunology, 90(3), 355-358. https://doi.org/10.1016/s1081-1206(10)61807-8

Gao Q, Kou T, Zhuang B, Ren Y, Dong X, Wang Q. The Association between Vitamin D Deficiency and Sleep Disorders: A Systematic Review and Meta-Analysis. Nutrients. 2018;10(10):1395. Published 2018 Oct 1. doi:10.3390/nu10101395

Guo J, Li L, Gong Y, et al. Massage Alleviates Delayed Onset Muscle Soreness after Strenuous Exercise: A Systematic Review and Meta-Analysis. Front Physiol. 2017;8:747. Published 2017 Sep 27. doi:10.3389/fphys.2017.00747

Hofmann, S., Asnaani, A., Vonk, I., Sawyer, A., & Fang, A. (2012). The Efficacy of Cognitive Behavioral Therapy: A Review of Meta-analyses. Cognitive Therapy And Research, 36(5), 427-440. https://doi.org/10.1007/s10608-012-9476-1

Ikonte, C., Mun, J., Reider, C., Grant, R., & Mitmesser, S. (2019). Micronutrient Inadequacy in Short Sleep: Analysis of the NHANES 2005–2016. Nutrients, 11(10), 2335. https://doi.org/10.3390/nu11102335

INAGAWA, K., HIRAOKA, T., KOHDA, T., YAMADERA, W., & TAKAHASHI, M. (2006). Subjective effects of glycine ingestion before bedtime on sleep quality. Sleep And Biological Rhythms, 4(1), 75-77. https://doi.org/10.1111/j.1479-8425.2006.00193.x

Lean, Geoffrey. "Mobile Phone Radiation Wrecks Your Sleep". The Independent, 2008, https://www.independent.co.uk/life-style/health-and-families/health-news/mobile-phone-radiation-wrecks-your-sleep-771262.html.

Linda Handlin, Eva Hydbring-Sandberg, Anne Nilsson, Mikael Ejdebäck, Anna Jansson & Kerstin Uvnäs-Moberg (2011) Short-Term Interaction between Dogs and Their Owners: Effects on Oxytocin, Cortisol, Insulin and Heart Rate—An Exploratory Study, Anthrozoös, 24:3, 301-315, DOI: 10.2752/175303711X13045914865385

Markil N, Whitehurst M, Jacobs PL, Zoeller RF. Yoga Nidra relaxation increases heart rate variability and is unaffected by a prior bout of Hatha

yoga. J Altern Complement Med. 2012;18(10):953-958. doi:10.1089/
acm.2011.0331

McGonigal, Kelly. (2012). The Willpower Instinct (p. 45). Avery.

Naik, G., Gaur, G., & Pal, G. (2018). Effect of Modified Slow Breathing
Exercise on Perceived Stress and Basal Cardiovascular Parameters.
International Journal Of Yoga, 11(1), 53-58. https://doi.org/10.4103/
ijoy.IJOY_41_16

Nam, H., Park, C., Crane, J., & Siebers, R. (2004). Endotoxin and House Dust
Mite Allergen Levels on Synthetic and Buckwheat Pillows. Journal Of
Korean Medical Science, 19(4), 505. https://doi.org/10.3346/
jkms.2004.19.4.505

National Safety Council. (2020). Drowsy Driving. Nsc.org. Retrieved from
https://www.nsc.org/road-safety/safety-topics/fatigued-driving.

National Sleep Foundation. (2020). CBT for Insomnia: Techniques & Case
Study - Sleep Foundation. Sleep Foundation. Retrieved from https://
www.sleepfoundation.org/articles/cognitive-behavioral-therapy-insomnia.

Noyek, S., Yaremchuk, K., & Rotenberg, B. (2016). Does melatonin have a
meaningful role as a sleep aid for jet lag recovery?. The Laryngoscope,
126(8), 1719-1720. https://doi.org/10.1002/lary.25689

Pereira N, Naufel MF, Ribeiro EB, Tufik S, Hachul H. Influence of Dietary
Sources of Melatonin on Sleep Quality: A Review. J Food Sci.
2020;85(1):5-13. doi:10.1111/1750-3841.14952

Regis W. Haid Jr., M. (2019). Acupressure: A Safe Alternative Therapy.
SpineUniverse. Retrieved from https://www.spineuniverse.com/treatments/
alternative/acupressure-safe-alternative-therapy.

Salcedo, S. (2019). How Heavy Should a Weighted Blanket Be? A Buying
Guide. Nectarsleep.com. Retrieved from https://www.nectarsleep.com/posts/
how-heavy-a-weighted-blanket-be/.

Schreiner, I., & Malcolm, J. (2008). The Benefits of Mindfulness Meditation:
Changes in Emotional States of Depression, Anxiety, and Stress. Behaviour
Change, 25(3), 156-168. https://doi.org/10.1375/bech.25.3.156

Schwecherl, L. (2017). 6 Benefits of Buckwheat Pillows | Sleepopolis. Sleepopolis. Retrieved from https://sleepopolis.com/blog/6-benefits-buckwheat-pillows/.

Spadola CE, Guo N, Johnson DA, et al. Evening intake of alcohol, caffeine, and nicotine: night-to-night associations with sleep duration and continuity among African Americans in the Jackson Heart Sleep Study. Sleep. 2019;42(11):zsz136. doi:10.1093/sleep/zsz136

Stevenson, S. (2016). Sleep Smarter. Rodale Books.

Taspinar, F., Aslan, U., Sabir, N., & Cavlak, U. (2013). Implementation of Matrix Rhythm Therapy and Conventional Massage in Young Females and Comparison of Their Acute Effects on Circulation. The Journal Of Alternative And Complementary Medicine, 19(10), 826-832. https://doi.org/10.1089/acm.2012.0932

UCLA. "Coping With Shift Work - UCLA Sleep Disorders Center - Los Angeles, CA". Uclahealth.Org, https://www.uclahealth.org/sleepcenter/coping-with-shift-work.

Walker, Matthew. Why We Sleep. Penguin Books, 2017

Wenninger, J., Meinitzer, A., Holasek, S. et al. Associations between tryptophan and iron metabolism observed in individuals with and without iron deficiency. Sci Rep 9, 14548 (2019). https://doi.org/10.1038/s41598-019-51215-8

YAMADERA, W., INAGAWA, K., CHIBA, S., BANNAI, M., TAKAHASHI, M., & NAKAYAMA, K. (2007). Glycine ingestion improves subjective sleep quality in human volunteers, correlating with polysomnographic changes. Sleep And Biological Rhythms, 5(2), 126-131. https://doi.org/10.1111/j.1479-8425.2007.00262.x

You Can Quit 2. How Nicotine Interferes with Sleep. You Can Quit 2. Retrieved 27 August 2020, from https://www.ycq2.org/tobacco-e-cigarettes/nicotine-and-sleep/.